Cambridge Elements ≡

Elements in Critical Heritage Studies
edited by
Kristian Kristiansen
University of Gothenburg
Michael Rowlands
UCL

T0286957

HERITAGE AND TRANSFORMATION OF AN AFRICAN POPULAR MUSIC

Aghi Bahi
The University of Félix-Houphouët-Boigny

CAMBRIDGE
UNIVERSITY PRESS

Heritage and Transformation of an African Popular Music

Elements in Critical Heritage Studies

DOI: 10.1017/9781009469159
First published online: December 2024

Aghi Bahi
The University of Félix-Houphouët-Boigny

Author for correspondence: Aghi Bahi, aghi.bahi@gmail.com

Abstract: Modern popular music is closely linked to the 'traditional' heritage – intangible and material – of which artist-musicians have, in a way, usufruct. This Element examines the relationship between (cultural) heritage and the transformation of popular music in Côte d'Ivoire. It views heritage from a dynamic and innovative perspective as a constantly evolving reality, informed by a multitude of encounters, both local and global. It frees itself from the sectoralisation and disciplinary impermeability of the sector – in places of music performance to understand how the artistic-musical heritage is transmitted, imagined and managed and in the complex process of transformation of popular music in which it registers. It appears that heritage, far from being frozen in time, is rather activated, deactivated and reactivated according to the creative imagination. In addition, the Element highlights a minor aspect of the heritage subsumed in popular intellectuality at work in popular music.

Keywords: heritage, modernity, popular music, traditions, popular culture

ISBNs: 9781009469180 (HB), 9781009469166 (PB), 9781009469159 (OC)
ISSNs: 2632-7074 (online), 2632-7066 (print)

Contents

'The strength of the baobab lies in its roots.'

– An African proverb

Introduction

In this Element, the question of heritage is explored from the vantage point of popular music in Côte d'Ivoire and, by extension or extrapolation, in Africa (see the following section). Côte d'Ivoire serves as a case study for a more productive approach to the question of heritage. The idea is simple: true African heritage is less a matter of *groove* than of popular intellectuality. This is where the authentic heritage of musical art in motion lies.

Popular Music and Heritage

Inheritance, here understood as what we have from predecessors, previous generations, and ancestors, in terms of character, ideology and so on (Larousse), implies 'cultural heritage' and appears as a synonym for 'tradition'. It then refers to (i) the set of legends, facts, doctrines, opinions, customs, usages and so on, transmitted orally over a long period of time; (ii) the ways of acting or thinking transmitted for generations within a group – denoted by the synonyms custom, practice, rite or usage. The concept of heritage is controversial, and what constitutes it is often contentious because of a reductive, Eurocentric legacy focused on the materiality that dominates thinking (Segobye 2007:79). Legacy can relate to both the tangible and the intangible, including 'intangible things such as ideas, or systems of knowledge' held and transmitted by various means from generation to generation, and in particular popular music.

In Africa, popular music is a kind of 'unifying syncretic framework' (Waterman 1990:376) that refers both to 'traditional', 'ethnic', 'people's' music, as well as to musical forms that are enjoyed or consumed by the population (Agawu 2016). The term popular refers to the realm of the culture of the oppressed and excluded classes (Hall 2007:77). In the field of arts and culture, specifically music, the notion of 'popular' is very broad, complex and rich, covering endogenous forms that continue to circulate but are not always visible. The field of popular music is broader than that restricted by the dominant conception of market exploitation. The dominant, even hegemonic idea of popular music is defined in dichotomous (or even contradictory) terms with respect to the music of the cultivated and/or westernised elite. Ivorian popular music has a relatively long history, and today's musicians are its heirs. The current world of 'postmodernity' (which thinks of itself as its own origin), with its linear conception of time, denies heritage (Paturet 2007; Lyotard 1979), as if the past were inevitably doomed to archaicness or tradition to immobility.

The global circulation of contemporary modern music (in all its forms) is such that it can be considered 'stateless' (Warnier 2007:3). It is therefore very difficult to locate modern popular music within the confines of the nation-state. However, the term is retained for practical reasons of feasibility. Moreover, music, like the cultures in which it is embedded, is 'singular, extraordinarily diverse and localised' (Warnier 2007:7). 'Popular' music is (therefore) (already) a mixture of diverse traditions and logics that remains open to continual enrichment. Today's dominant popular music is (therefore) only a reduced aspect of the ontological reality of popular music. The conception of modern popular music used in our approach and referred to here is a much more 'complete' version than the dominant (and hegemonic) one. Rather, it is understood as a version at the intersection of the popular (as defined earlier) and the market (Waterman 1990).

Popular music in Côte d'Ivoire is the subject of growing interest, but scientific production is having difficulty meeting the demand for knowledge in this fast-moving field. Some works, which tend to be journalistic, provide testimonial data on musicians and performance venues, offer anecdotes and confidences from artists, and shed light on their civic and political commitments in the light of their personal histories (Briard 2008; Babi 2010; Koffi et al. 2022). The dominant trend in scholarly works is to focus on one genre (or even one style) or on one artist embodying one genre or another, while at the same time paying homage to these icons of urban popular music. Specific works – on Dan music (Zemp 1971[2012]), the *tohourou bété* (Wondji 1986a, 1986b; Séry 2015) or the didactics of music teaching (Goran 2011) – do exist and act as pioneers.

However, the strong tendency towards sectorisation and disciplinary water-tightness means that most of the exegeses of the songs are contextualised as an introduction to the political sociology and recent history of Côte d'Ivoire. *Reggae*, for example, through its most prominent West African figures, Alpha Blondy and Tiken Jah Fakoly, has been approached from the point of view of the thoughts they convey and the effects these have on the future of the country and even the continent (Konaté 1987; Briard 2008; Brou 2018a, 2018b; Koffi et al. 2022). The *zouglou* musical genre, the visible face of social and political demands, has been the subject of a multi-biographical approach to the famous group Magic System (Vergès 2018), or, with the Yodé and Siro affair, from the angle of its tumultuous relationship with political power (Bahi 2021; Kadi 2021). The analysis of the rise of the *coupé décalé*, an urban music genre characteristic of the 2000s (Kolé 2023), focuses in particular on Douk Saga and DJ Arafat, emblematic figures of the genre (Boka 2013; Guébo 2022). The introduction of *pop music* in Côte d'Ivoire, its reception and the development of its local variant complete the panorama (Djédjé 2020). Most of the time, therefore, these local works focus on a particular musical genre (or style), or a particular artist (modern or traditional), from a certain period or currently in vogue, creating magnifying glass effects and ipso facto obliterating the possibility of a global grasp of the phenomenon.

Heritage at Risk?

More general work was begun in the 1980s (Wondji 1986a, 1986b; Konaté 1987). They approach the various genres (and styles) of Ivorian popular music in the same phenomenal way. The issues of immediate sociopolitical change in Côte d'Ivoire, closely linked to the armed rebellion of 2002 and the electoral crisis of 2010 that led to the tragic events we know about (Fié Doh 2012), are bringing popular music into conversation with political 'conscientisation' (Bahi 2021). The question of cultural heritage and the mutations of popular music timidly appears from the angle of the impending disappearance of the *tohourou* genre under the impact of Western culture (Wondji 1986a, 1986b; Séry 2015). Inheritance/heritage is treated from the perspective of destruction, if not imminent then at least imminent in line with the spirit animating certain literary and ethnological studies of the twentieth century, and with a conservatory aim, clinging to a melancholy reminiscence of the past (Wondji 1986a, 1986b; Babi 2010; Séry 2015). In the background, culture, conceived as a fixed entity, is under attack from Western culture and is in danger of disappearing.

Inheritance seems commonly (implicitly) conceived as an anonymous thing of the past or even of tradition, relatively stationary, transmissible to its legitimate heirs without alteration or modification, thus inducing a relatively rigid posture (e.g. Kebede 1982; Olaniyan 2004; Agawu 2016). The question of inheritance is linked to those of heritage preservation, (cultural) identity and authenticity/originality. African composers, in a process of innovation attempting to set themselves apart from Western or Euro-American artistic flows, use 'the materials of their indigenous musical traditions' and would give priority 'to the propagation and enhancement of its heritage rather than to musical originality' (Kebede 1982:118).

The preservation of an artistic heritage cannot be reduced to its stereotypical reproduction (Waterman 1990:377). The use of 'traditional' musical instruments cannot in itself establish the authenticity of a musical work. 'Authentic' music does not reside exclusively in Indigenous forms. Heritage can be manipulated according to whether the conception of identity is narrow or broad, closed or open. Authenticity, which is always relative, limited and dependent on the outside world, ultimately translates into a 'cosmopolitan nativism' (Olaniyan 2004), which is not folded into an Indigenous ancestrality, but is open to intentional and egalitarian hybridisation. In resistance to domination, it also appears as 'a powerful stimulant and rallying cry [for identity]' (Olaniyan 2004:165). The African 'past' and its traditions, the ancestral heritage, thus appear to be both a site of polemic and a source of replenishment, 'a potential capital for improvement' (Olaniyan 2004:158–159). The African composer's artistic heritage is said to have three origins: (i) the various Indigenous traditions, including rumba and its offshoots; (ii) Europe, distilled through religious and military music; and (iii) the Western avant-garde (Agawu 2016).

Modern popular music, in its marketing version, 'absorbs' the 'traditional' (or so-called traditional music), the 'ethnic', and claims its originality on this basis, in order to gain visibility and an audience. So it is not a question of relying on a divide between 'elite music' and 'popular music', or on a 'rupture' between 'traditional' and 'modern', but rather on grasping the places of exchange and conversation, of complementarity between these polarities (Waterman 1990; Olaniyan 2004). How can we understand and show how musics enrich each other? How does modern popular music draw on this fund (which itself is not static)? How, in return, does 'traditional' ('ethnic') music 'survive', change and adapt to the new situation?

Rethinking Heritage

Beyond the relatively rigid posture of an immutable past (Kebede 1982; Agawu 2016), we can in fact, more productively, think of heritage in a more dynamic and fertile conception. This question of heritage can be approached by attempting to articulate historical, ethnographic and anthropological approaches under the influence of (British) *cultural studies*, while benefiting from the renewal of musicology (e.g. Waterman 1990; Olaniyan 2004; Agawu 2016). In fact, traditional and modern are part of a relationship of continuity and are intertwined (Waterman 1990:368). Artistic and musical creation does not happen ex nihilo. It is necessarily engaged in inter-musical relations, particularly with precursors, 'whether in affirmation or dissent, actively or passively, consciously or unconsciously' (Agawu 2016:315). Fundamentally, the musical composer, in exercising his artistic freedom of thought, navigates between aesthetic canons to be respected and transgressions – an exercise in unstable equilibrium without which musical art ultimately does not exist and thanks to which the unexpected happens.

Heritage is seen as a constantly evolving reality, informed by a multitude of encounters, both local and global. It is constantly negotiated in the present and in the future. Its ethnographic present is part of a kind of ongoing past. The heritage is not (un)past, it is not in rupture. By freeing ourselves from a linear conception of time, we can say: 'Inheritance comes to us from the depths of our future' (Paturet 2007:25), because the heirs also have the task of giving consistency to the outline that has been passed on to them, of taking charge of the inheritance and extending the gesture: 'Inheriting is therefore not about "breaking away" from the "past", but on the contrary about "becoming part of the chain of history" and "taking charge" of the values transmitted, by constituting oneself as the inventor or creator' (Paturet 2007:26).

Heritage does not obstruct the possibility of invention or innovation, quite the contrary. Rather than a radical break between 'traditional' music and modern popular music, I defend the thesis of a cultural heritage inscribed in a continuity between these two artistic expressions: modern popular music is closely linked to the 'traditional' heritage (immaterial and material) of which the artist-musicians have a sort of usufruct. There is a continuity from 'traditional music' to modern popular music, which is certainly a legacy. Music is also part of the intangible heritage (Rowlands 2008) and even of the 'places' of sound memory (Agawu 2016:4). The past lives in the present, says Maurice Godelier (2015). It could even be said that the present draws on the past to innovate ... The past is therefore not a subject of 'archaism' but rather a place of resourcing (Waterman 1990).

Inheritance is not frozen in time. It is activated, deactivated and reactivated at the whim of the creative imagination. This imagination also follows the paths of cannibalism. The practice of cannibalism is an insidious part of everyday life and social processes (Nyamnjoh 2018:5). The human being, fundamentally incomplete, is inscribed in relationships of cannibalistic reciprocity with the other (Nyamnjoh 2018). The creative imagination, in order to innovate and/or be authentic, original, and so on, can take the form of 'a productive, invigorating and crucial form of cannibalism' (Nyamnjoh 2018:10). This artistic-musical cannibalism is reflected in the various cover versions, remixes, and so on, that have been made. The 'tradi-moderne', a form of cannibalisation of the 'traditional', represents this continuity between the traditional and the modern while cornering its market. The question of musical heritage is also linked to that of copyright in 'traditional' musical heritage or materials derived from traditional musical heritage (Barber 2015). The problem of the use of traditional materials in popular (or learned) musical compositions is becoming increasingly acute.

The Authentic Place of Heritage

The heritage lies as much in the (popular) intellectuality conveyed by the music as in the traditional materials that can be freely plundered. The often paradoxical popular intellectuality of musical artists is symptomatic of the aporias of the post-colonial African state and of cultural production in post-coloniality. This produces a complex subject, subject to an exotic (imported), inauthentic, accessory or optional symbolic economy, generally perceived as subornation, limiting our autonomy (Olaniyan 2004:165). But by revisiting (and recycling) these traditional materials, a genuine source of originality, modern popular music reveals, preserves and (re)brings to life the musical heritage in cannibalistic fashion. In the artistic and musical world, the custodians of vulnerable tradition are being cannibalised in the face of neoliberal modernisation characterised by industrialisation, commodification, consumerism, globalisation and trivialisation (Nyamnjoh 2018:2–3). Traditional precursor artist-musicians are thus 'cannibalised' without any acknowledgement of debt (Nyamnjoh 2018). 'Tradition' is thus the well that feeds 'modernity'. 'Modern' creation draws from 'traditions' and is replenished by them in this symbolic cannibalism.

Modern popular music is closely linked to the market (music marketing in this case) and to the mass media that ensure its visibility (Thomas & Nyamnjoh 2007; Diawarra 2015). As an object of research, it is stretched between the local (in terms of situations and places) and the global (in terms of economic, political and social systems), between instances of musical production and instances of reception and effects of music (Rouzé 2004:11). Even under colonial rule, the music of the colonised did not always conform to the exogenously generated logics of colonial power and capitalism. This is why, beyond the elite/people distinction, it is important to pay attention to the field generally referred to as traditional and endogenous music. The artist-musicians who have responded to the call of commercialism and the commodification of their works have tended (to draw inspiration from or) to borrow from various market musical traditions: ethnic, popular, elitist, colonial and Western. Artists also draw on popular music in their quest for creativity and originality. On the other hand, 'ethnic' and 'traditional' music continues to live on by borrowing from the dominant forms of music on the market. Today, popular music is a cultural commodity integrated into the market economy, particularly the globalised entertainment economy (Flichy 1991; Rouzé 2004).

Methodological Note

This Element is based on previous anthropological fieldwork, flirting with the anthropology of the city, and paying attention to cultural diversity in a comprehensive approach, in an attempt to grasp the meaning of the other by empathising with their experience and interpreting their intention or intentionality. It focuses specifically on modern popular music in Côte d'Ivoire, as a cultural institution. The question of heritage is examined through the logic and modalities of its production, its actors, its places of performance (rehearsal rooms, recording studios, etc.), and so on. The data come from a multi-site survey (by impregnation, in situ observation) of informants from the world of producers (creators, singers, arrangers, studio technicians, etc.) in their places of work, their frame of ordinary experience (Goffman 1991). In Abidjan (Côte d'Ivoire), this survey consisted of meeting musicians who were members of groups in training that *were* ideologically opposed, but which were similar in terms of their socioeconomic and working conditions: young musicians who tended to play *zouglou*, others who claimed to be *Rastas,* musicians who were labelled *jazz* but who moved happily from one musical style to another. These groups of young people are windows onto the elective communities or 'tribes' (Maffesoli 1988) that populate the music world and enliven the local musical scene. As far as possible, the deterritorialised view took in the various performance venues of the players and, at the same time, the critical venues of musical mediation. These are places of creation (young *zouglou, rasta* and *jazz* musicians, rehearsal rooms, etc.), places of production (studio, 'producer's' office) and so on. The oral dimension is inevitably linked to the popular nature of this music. Admittedly, it is important to avoid the aporia of 'graphocentrism', so it should come as no surprise that there are no musical transcriptions in this Element. The work also necessitated a historiography based on a social history on the fringes of a (controversial) history of the present day: 'that which is done with and under the control of witnesses, it is also that which can use their contribution to make up for the absence of scriptural sources and to constitute others that allow history to be written differently' (Wolikow 1998:14).

Outlines

The Element is divided into eight sections. The first three deal with the rise of modern popular music in a kind of archaeology of recent history. This elementary historicisation has made it possible to contextualise contemporary Ivorian popular music. Localised music, in other places, in other (cultural) flows, comes, forms and mixes to create as much as possible these *mediascapes* or *ideoscapes* (Appadurai 2001) – or, to push the same logic, *soundscapes* or even *musicscapes*, for purposes of contextualisation. The Element then turns to the poetics of contemporary urban musical art in Côte d'Ivoire. The following four sections examine this social phenomenon from the angle of its creation, performance, learning and ritualisation (its social functions), in its political, social and cultural contexts. Technology is important. It largely determines the production and inevitably the form and content of music. Here too, it is important to avoid the trap of 'technologism'. Finally, popular music today is (much) more than technology. The final section examines what constitutes the true meaning of the artistic-musical heritage: modern popular music is difficult to restrain. Deployed between entertainment and popular intellectuality, is it not the place of heritage par excellence?

A brief history of the rise of Ivorian popular music can first be understood in the context of the peri-Atlantic circulation of people, ideas and objects. It is then written in the more localised context of such movements on the West African coast and in the colonies. In this way, the dominant or hegemonic urban musical forms were created and developed in the city, from colonisation to the twenty-first century. This history enables us to understand the profound consequences that the past has had on the recent form, content and direction of popular music. 'We sit on the old mat to weave the new one'. The contemporary city preserves and reinforces these attributes. We will show how Ivorian popular music has become a (quasi-)cultural industry.

1 Popular Music in the Colony

During the colonial period, the music of Africans changed, 'asserted itself and diversified' (Wondji 1986a:14) through contact with the burgeoning city, the small proletariat that developed there, the youth associations and movements (Mignon 1984:68) active in working-class neighbourhoods, urban festivals, bar-dancings (Balandier 1957; Rouch 1959), thanks to the development and expansion of sound broadcasting (Tudesq 1998) and above all the record industry and the gradual replacement of the gramophone by the electrophone and the tape recorder. The city in Côte d'Ivoire is a 'product of colonisation' (Zadi 1990:31), determining its population, morphology, physiognomy and sociology. The structuring of urban space between 1920 and 1930 was to have a lasting impact on the subsequent urbanisation of Côte d'Ivoire. The urban centre developed by the coloniser was the territorial framework around which new economic structures were organised and articulated (Kipré 1975:102–107).

Aimed at satisfying the needs of the metropolis, the economy of the colony of Côte d'Ivoire combined the pre-colonial cycles of production and trade with a trading economy characterised by the export of 'very heavy raw products (wood, cocoa, palm oil and palm kernels in particular, but also kola); in return it received finished products whose weight was much less important than their price' (Kipré 1975:100). The colonial context, which turned ancient African society upside down, was therefore a decisive turning point in the evolution and transformation of music.

The colonial period was the time when African societies learned to live in cities. The initial difficulties in populating the city gave way to workers' camps, designed for young men who had a job and were assumed to be single. The regrouping or formation of families then made it possible to rebalance and broaden the age pyramids at the base. (Piermay 2003:39)

In the coastal towns in particular, dealing with European ships, ordinary social and cultural life was altered. These towns were 'active markets for foodstuffs and imported consumer goods' (Kipré 1975:116). After 1930, the small towns of Côte d'Ivoire had a heterogeneous African social environment made up of business-men, landowners, traders, urban planters, large traders, civil servants and factory clerks. This sort of literate urban bourgeoisie was distinguished from the rest of the African population by its remuneration and civic status (Kipré 1986; Le Pape 1997). This social milieu soon saw a mixture of native, non-native and non-Indigenous populations made up of employees, shopkeepers and craftsmen who quickly formed the small proletariat of the cities and who were the real inhabitants of the city, appropriating this space and organising its social and cultural life (Wondji 1986a:19).

The city, its movement and circulation, brought about changes in forms of sociality, in systems of representation and in individual behaviour (Bibeau 1993:254). These embryonic multi-ethnic cities mixed ethnic groups from within and outside the colony: 'through maritime navigation and colonial routes, people and techniques moved, as did cultural and artistic modes' (Wondji 1986a: 19). Music from elsewhere, from Europe, continental Africa and the diaspora, was heard and developed in the new cities. Musical practices in West and Southern Africa in the nineteenth century were already marked by exchanges and mixtures with those of Europe, the Caribbean and the Americas. Congolese rumba, which was to influence popular music in Côte d'Ivoire, was one of the fruits of these exchanges (see Doua 2020:160).

The city was a key venue for the dissemination of music from the African diaspora in the Americas, creating new, essentially crossbred musical forms which, by crossing 'the Atlantic once again, but in the opposite direction, [contributed] to the genesis of new African popular music, which the Congo of the time had specialised in' (Bonniol 1999:321). In short, 'the city was a fertile cultural melting pot where different musical genres collided and interpenetrated' (Meyran 2014:2).

The bars and dance halls, mixing crowds and sounds, are undeniably import-ant in the social life of the African city of its birth (Balandier 1957:283–284). The novel *Ville cruelle* (*Cruel City*) describes how, at nightfall, the hub of life shifts from the administrative centre to the outlying districts, constituting a 'revenge' of the Indigenous quarter on the European quarter (Eza Boto 1954[1971]:23). The film *Moi un Noir* (*Me a Black*) (Rouch 1959) introduces us to the contrasting arcana of Abidjan, a 'holiday town' for Europeans at the end of the colonial period, showing the nightlife in Treichville and the bustling cultural scene. In bars such as *L'Etoile du sud*, *Le Tourlourou*, *L'Espérance* and *L'Oasis du désert*, Caribbean *cha cha* was fashionable and Congolese *rumba* was beginning to make inroads, performed by local orchestras. The modern popular music that emerged developed in an urban environment, on the outskirts of the city of the whites, in a phenomenon shared by the French colonies (Balandier 1957; Rouch 1959; Gondola 2003, 1997; Kouvouama 2013). In the colonial city, in fact, 'popular song developed within the immigrant African communities that took charge of creating a specifically African urban culture' (Wondji 1986a:19; see also Le Pape 1997).

In the city, [modern] popular song also developed 'within the immigrant African communities who took charge of the creation of a specifically African urban culture' (Wondji 1986a:19). Until the early 1950s, the secondary sector was still in its infancy, and the majority of the population had not broken with peasant life. Thus, there was no difference between the oral poetry (declaimed or sung) practised in town and that of the countryside (Zadi 1990:32). These 'traditional' forms of poetry were to change as a result of contact with French chanson and music and aesthetics from elsewhere. But the real turning point came when Congolese orchestras, particularly OK Jazz, toured Côte d'Ivoire. 'The neo-oralist movement was born and soon established its own celebrities: Nahounou Digbeu, known as Amédée Pierre, Anouma Brouh Félix, Mamadou Doumbia, Ndouba Simon, and later Ernesto Djédjé, father of modern Ziglibity, and many others' (Zadi 1990:32). Amédée Pierre, the paragon of the modern singer, took up the 'traditionality' of the 'traditional' singer, brought about a veritable revolution in sung poetry by using the Bété language and modern musical orchestration, and 'succeeded in recreating in the city, among a population that did not speak the same language, the village poetry evenings that seemed to suit only small, linguistically unified communities' (Zadi 1990:33).

The arrival of electricity had an impact on both the city and the production and consumption of music. Phonographs – the privilege of wealthy citizens, clubs and bars – and later electrophones and tape recorders, as well as the development of sound broadcasting around the world and the introduction of radio in Côte d'Ivoire were to broaden the audience for Western popular music and that of the Black Atlantic. Thanks to the boom in maritime transport, objects (78 rpm records from the Black Americas, musical instruments) of knowledge and know-how from the Black Americas were introduced by Latin American sailors – Cubans in particular, and Krou sailors (Gondola 1997; Mazzoleni 2010). Transport and (means of) communication were therefore of vital importance in this circulation of cultural products (Warnier 2007:28–29; Gilroy 2010), but also of musical ideas, learning, inspiration and artistic emulation, as the example of Wendo Kolosoy shows (Popovitch 1992). The colonial period also saw the development of brass bands, the first of which were military or militarised, pastiches of *marching bands* or *brass bands*, circulating initially along the Ivorian coast (Dagri 2019a).

Music is created and developed through a 'circulation' of knowledge and know-how, motifs (themes), harmonic sequences, sonorities, instruments, cadences, rhythms and rhythmic forms, and so on. Former American slaves were to become formidable sailors in the European fleets, as well as musicians who were to deploy their talents wherever they went, particularly in Sierra Leone and Côte d'Ivoire. It was in this context that the brass band took off, particularly in the circles of Grand-Béréby, Tabou, Sassandra, and Fresco (Dagri 2019a). This cultural 'graft' took hold for cultural, social and religious reasons. On the coast, where the colonial presence was strong, colonisation intentionally destroyed the Indigenous cultures and substituted its own. Music in particular, an important element of cultural identity, was disqualified in favour of fanfare music performed at official and public events. For its part, the Catholic Church outlawed certain Indigenous practices, including the playing of traditional musical instruments (Nyamnjoh & Fokwang 2005).

The creation of African brass bands and the creation of 'Indigenous' repertoires is often a reaction to this negation of 'Indigenous' music by the colonisers. Throughout the coast, the brass band has become a 'tradition' and the local populations have conceivably 'forgotten' traditional music as it might have been played with the traditional instruments of the *Kroumen*, *Néyo* and so on. It can be assumed that they have certainly reflected their habitus of playing traditional music. We can assume that they have certainly translated their musical habitus into Western tempered instruments and harmonic structures.

In the second half of the nineteenth century, Jamaican sailors began spreading Caribbean music (i.e. *calypso*, *merengue*) in Cape Town (South Africa). These styles spread up and down the West African coast, mixing with other local rhythms by river and land, producing such novelties as the *adaha*, an African brass band. Later, in the 1920s, in Sierra Leone, the *Kru* sailors, of good repute, returned from coastal trading in the Congo with alcohol, but also with melodies, musical instruments and the rudiments of instrumental technique (Doumergue 1981). They created a (*softer*) derivative of the *adaha*, the *maringa*, a '*palm wine jazz*', played on guitars, banjos and accordions, combining the songs and dances of the English sailors with Caribbean melodies such as *foxtrot* and *calypso*, giving rise to other types of music (Collins 1992). This palm wine music was adopted and spread by the *Kru* sailors from Liberia sailing along the West African coast. In the process, they also spread guitars, banjos and accordions throughout the coastal countries, as far as Cape Town. In the mid-1920s, this new music (*maringa*) reached Ghana where, mixing with *osibisaba*, a *Fanti* rhythm, *foxtrot*, *palm wine jazz* and so on, it developed in the 1930s and 1940s into *highlife*, a fusion of black American, European and African music, popularised in the following years.

The port cities, often former colonial trading posts that gave rise to large cities and important ports, ensured the circulation of musical instruments and technical devices. This aspect of Atlantic circulation plays an important role in understanding the dynamics of the creation of new music and new cultures in continental Africa (Zeleza 2005:221), and in Côte d'Ivoire in particular. It enables us to understand the birth of Congolese *highlife* and *rumba*, which were to have a major influence on the creation of modern Ivorian popular music. In the end, whatever the mode, musical 'traditions' blend together to produce the multi-traditional cultural fund from which contemporary creation draws. The circuits of influence seem to form part of an endless circularity.

In the 1950s (until the end of the 1960s), popular balls – the famous 'dust balls' – were predominant, often led by 'ethnic' orchestras. The adventure of radio broadcasting in Côte d'Ivoire began in 1949. It had only been possible to establish radio broadcasting 'since the popularisation of transistor radios' (Tudesq 2002:5). The period of independence coincided with the invention of the transistor. At the same time as the voice of political leaders, modern popular song could begin to penetrate the countryside as well as the city. Radio was as much a vehicle for African nationalism, particularly that of Kwame Nkrumah (in 1957) and Sékou Touré (in 1958), neighbours of Félix Houphouët-Boigny's Côte d'Ivoire, as it was for popular song. It was through them that the famous *'Indépendance cha cha'* (by Grand Kallé and African Jazz) was popularised. But also, in a post-war context, where the Ivorian political system was initiating the industrialisation of the country, the question of mass culture inevitably arose. Society was no longer restricted to the literate urban elite, but was gradually expanding to include more modest sections of the population (the urban proletariat, the rural petty bourgeoisie, etc.). These groups, excluded from the modern society that was taking shape, found 'forms of belonging and cultural forms' in a popular culture that was itself under construction (compare Balandier 1955; Rouch 1959). With the rise of radio broadcasting in the late 1950s (Tudesq 1998, 1999, 2002; Bahi 1998; Koné 1989), that of cinema (Retord 1986; Traoré 1986) and then that of terrestrial television (Koné 1989; Bahi 1994, 1998, 1999) from 1963 onwards, of the press and in particular magazines, with the introduction of images from the Western world, from the end of the 1960s in the case of Côte d'Ivoire, communication opened up the market for leisure activities and cultural industries (Caune 1995:44).

In Côte d'Ivoire, *highlife* music, the official national music of Ghana, first influenced Christian religious singing (prosaically known as church music). *Highlife* (and Afro-Cuban music) reached Central Africa in the 1950s and had an impact on Congolese *rumba*. In the Belgian Congo, it influenced Wendo Kolosoy, one of the pioneers of Congolese *rumba*. The influence of West African immigrants, who were 'advanced' musically, brought their know-how (the *highlife* in vogue at the time) to musicians in Central Africa, thus influencing *rumba*. Their 'advance' was probably due to the fact that Africans, Ghanaians in particular, had been drafted into European armies during the pre-colonial era, but especially during the colonial period. They were thus exposed to military musical traditions (Dagri 2019a). Karin Barber (2018) sums up this whole period well, and what she says about colonial sub-Saharan Africa applies to the situation in Côte d'Ivoire at the time:

> In almost every city in colonial sub-Saharan Africa, new genres of popular music emerged: *highlife* on the Gold Coast, *juju* in western Nigeria, Congolese rumba, *dansi* in Dar es Salaam, *marabi*, *kwela* and *isicathamiya* in South Africa. Increasingly, in the mid-twentieth century, the popular music movement took on an extra dimension: radio, then television, gave it a wider reach and faster movement. New popular styles crossed national borders and new songs conquered audiences in entire regions with extraordinary speed. But underneath it all, live bands travelled from town to town and records, and later cassettes, were distributed along the roads and railways from town to town and from cities to small towns and villages. It seems that new styles were forged in specific urban centres and moved, adapting as they went, to other places. (p. 99)

The term 'jazz', a sign of the influence of North American music from the 1950s onwards, is a true symbol of the modernity of African musicians and orchestras today (Mazzoleni 2010). Understanding this Ivorian popular music requires us to articulate the rural and urban worlds, not in a dichotomous juxtaposition or antinomy, but rather in terms of poles of tension and complementarity. Instead, their relationship should be understood in terms of 'rurbanity', the interface that is created when they meet. Rurbanity is understood as an intermediate space between town and country, between urban and rural. Rural people moving to the city in defined areas, urban people moving to the village in defined areas, all play an equally important role in the creation of rurbanity. It is a transitional space between urban and rural lifestyles, a place of mixing and compromise. The heuristic scope of the category 'rurbanité' seems to us to be more productive in that it emphasises an intermediate reality, one that defines the terms 'urban' and 'rural' not in terms of oppositions but rather in terms of complementarity.

Modern popular music is first and foremost a product of 'rurbanity'. The 'rurban' space is understood as a place at the heart of the everyday life we live, and 'where the unfinished spatial dynamics of centrality are inscribed' (Bachimon 2001:10). The 'rurban' space, then, refers to those – often diffuse – places where town and country intertwine from a geographical, social, cultural, in short anthropological point of view, where modernity is negotiated (Macamo 2005), where it is constructed daily in a processual way in the acts of ordinary individuals. Modern popular music therefore also develops in the rurban enclaves of cities undergoing rapid transformation (Rouch 1957, 1959). It is born of the meeting of worlds, as sketched out again in the film *La pyramide humaine* (Rouch 1959). This place allows us to grasp the very birth of rhythms and sounds, poetic and choreographic expressions, the transformations of existing musical art forms and the creativity induced by the city (Bibeau 1993:255; Roskem 2014).

The burgeoning city was already an effervescent place where diverse cultural realities rubbed shoulders, where musical genres and styles developed, echoed and exchanged. Music travels, 'knows no boundaries', knows how to ignore territories and create new ones (Lafannour 2003). It is built on the circulation of ideas, musical concepts and objects; on blending (on 'miscegenation', creolisation), on cultural plurality, and is therefore mestizo by essence. It has to be said, then, that modern Ivorian popular music takes off through and in the movement of people, ideas and objects. It sounds like a pastiche of the observations made by Claude Lévi-Strauss in *Anthropologie structurale* (1958[1974]), in particular the exchange of people, goods and messages.

2 The Development of (and by) Popular Music

Independence in French-speaking sub-Saharan Africa was marked by the famous '*Independence cha cha*'. This reappropriation of an 'essentially' African rhythm, (re-)formed in the Americas and the Caribbean and brought back to Africa thanks to maritime transport, the phonograph, the nascent record industry and embryonic radio broadcasting, closely associated with urbanisation (Nyamnjoh & Fokwang 2005:254), is of undeniable symbolic significance. Indeed, 'during the Second World War, more difficult relations with the metropolis led African stations to produce more local broadcasts' (Tudesq 1998:59–60). Despite the work of balkanisation and the strengthening of national sentiment brought about by the slow establishment of territorial radio stations, it is conceivable that modern popular music has remained extraterritorial. Concerning an administrative, social and cultural whole much larger than that of the (sometimes shifting) borders of a particular colony, popular music carries the hopes of development and the dreams of modernism of this young Africa.

At the beginning of the African rumba musical adventure, local rumba performers had to give the impression that they were speaking Spanish. This produced a kind of onomatopoeia that was often grotesque but that created the illusion of singing in Spanish. And even if this babble had no name, it was reminiscent of '*fonronfifon naspa*' or 'tirailleurs' French', the illusion of speaking the dominant 'civilised' French language (Hampâté Bâ 1992:148). Later, as *pop music* spread over radio, television and dance halls, the illusion was that of speaking English, or even American. On reflection, this is reminiscent of the film *Moi un Noir,* in which Tarzan the Taxi Driver gabbles something that is supposed to be the English of American action films and, above all, the accent of Lemmy Caution, 'American federal agent'.

In the first decade of independence (1960–1970), the newly independent Côte d'Ivoire had no cultural policy and even less of a real vision for modern popular music. It was building its cultural autonomy on the basis of material from colonial times, but also from mixing with other cultures. Yet music seemed to define a consumer market. In the early 1960s, Côte d'Ivoire imported cameras and accessories, phonographs, *pick-ups*, motors, record players, record changers, and so on from Switzerland, at least 50 per cent of them for cinema equipment (projectors and cameras). In music in particular: *rumba, highlife,* French 'sentimental' music, and so on. This process of recycling also reflects a process of identity-building through music.

In the 1970s, Côte d'Ivoire tried to follow this trend with the creation of major orchestras, such as the Orchestre national directed by Joseph Pango, the Orchestre de la Radiodiffusion télévision ivoirienne (ORTI), and orchestras such as the OFI de Bouaké and Le Bélier Andralex. Independence accelerated and amplified this movement initiated by the colonial situation. There is undoubtedly a close link between urban development and popular music. 'The post-colonial phase [of the city] is that of the massification of the city, but also that of the appropriation of the city by African societies' (Piermay 2003:39). With the possible exception of Plateau, all of Abidjan's neighbourhoods are characterised by precarious housing, cosmopolitanism and intermingling, and are in a sense a 'detribalised' environment (Yapi Diahou 2000: 125–134). These 'zones' are not, therefore, watertight, but are places par excellence of cultural exchange and mixing (Wondji 1986a, Kipré 1985, Yapi Diahou 2000). In addition, economic growth has led to 'a massive rural exodus and intense immigration from neighbouring countries' (Wondji 1986a:21). School enrolment provided a stimulus for modernisation. But schooling is not enough to satisfy the cultural needs, which have increased or are increasing, and which reflect the spiritual void. This spiritual emptiness is due to a propensity to enjoy material wealth and the hunger to consume engendered by modern society. Côte d'Ivoire is entering a consumer society. Song attempts to fill this cultural and spiritual void by expressing the aspirations of the masses: freedom, justice, solidarity, social progress. While modernising (in terms of instrumentation, structuring, harmonisation and composition), it valued the national languages through which it often expressed itself, improved knowledge of the past, and gave impetus to the cultural dynamic which itself accompanied the social and economic (political?) dynamic (Wondji 1986a:21).

Independent Côte d'Ivoire witnessed a profusion of rhythms and songs, 'a "national surge" in popular song', with 'singers from all ethnic groups appearing on the Ivorian musical scene, stimulated by the development of modern means of expressing and disseminating music' (Wondji 1986a:14). There was a veritable flowering of artists and icons of the Ivorian musical universe, and Abidjan evenings were divided between numerous bars, *nightclubs* and *dance halls*.

This does not mean that 'traditional' popular music has disappeared. Local, typical music is developing and even showing a certain vitality. 'Traditional' artists are evolving year after year in the new world of *show business* and the music industry. In more prosaic terms, the various genres and styles of popular music are categorised according to ethnic criteria ('bété', 'attié', 'dioula', etc.) or regional criteria ('western', 'Agnéby', 'mandingue', etc.). These many qualifications do little to hide the difficulty of classifying musical genres that are in fact already and always mixtures. The concept of 'tradi-moderne' put forward by musicologists and cultural journalists aims to characterise music that takes its inspiration from traditional music and interprets it with modern musical instruments (Kua-Nzambi Toko 2018) in order to account for the complementarity of these incompleteness (to take up Nyamnjoh 2017's proposal).

The emergence of certain figures in African popular music and a number of events have certainly influenced sub-Saharan artists. In the 1960s, musicians from the two Congos, the flagships of Congolese rumba, were to have a certain influence on Ivorian music. Events in Côte d'Ivoire itself and elsewhere in Africa were to shake up the music scene and influence Ivorian musical creativity. While many Ivorian decision-makers considered music to be mere entertainment, or even an obstacle to development (Dagri 2019b), President Félix Houphouët-Boigny saw it as a soft power tool, part of his development showcase and an ideology of success capable of attracting foreign investment. The country became more open to foreign artistic influences, continuing a movement that had begun during the colonial era.

In the 1970s, thanks to the penetration of radio, the development of television and the spread of vinyl records across the country, the ears and eyes of young people in Abidjan became more open to world music. Radio Côte d'Ivoire kept the airwaves alive with songs by French, African, American and Caribbean artists, who would have a strong influence on Ivorian musicians. Television broadcasts of French and American variety shows, as well as festivals and musical performances of various origins (including, for example, *Rumble in the Jungle* – the famous Ali–Foreman boxing match). Print magazines such as *Hit Parade* and *Salut les copains* circulated year in, year out, chronicling the lives of these new European idols, who were, after all, marked by a certain media Americanness. The mass media played a full part in this aesthetic openness, this cultural mix, in short, this circulation. Youth orchestras were influenced by the waves of '*yéyé*' (Morin 1962), *pop*, *rock*, *soul* and *jerk*, while others were influenced by Latin American rhythms. Ivorian popular music was influenced by rhythms from the Black African diaspora, particularly Cuban salsa, which began to develop in the 1960s. As if in response to a globalised movement (even if the term was not used at the time), young Ivorians mixed the *bit-nick ethos*, then the *hippy ethos*, with their African identity. They imitated these *pop music* figures and reproduced their music before producing '*Ivorian rock*'.

At the same time, in line with a trend that began during colonisation, major orchestras such as Les Grands Columbia d'Adzopé and TP audiorama orchestra, with big names such as Okoi Séka Athanase and Amédée Pierre, who continued to entertain (until the mid 1980s) at the L'Oasis dance hall in Treichville, were developed and maintained.

The modernisation of popular music continued, with an all-out search for new sounds drawn from the music (instruments, rhythms, melodies) of the Ivorian musical traditions, the music of the 'terroirs': 'modernisation' and even revolution in a certain sense of Ivorian music, but also hybridisation and the influence of hybrid music. This period also saw the development of so-called typical music, strongly influenced by jazz but above all by Congolese, Cuban and Ghanaian rumbas, known as *highlife* (Bemba 1984:46–47).

Abidjan was more than just a stopover for visiting musicians; it was a place where music could flourish, and one that also played a part in the transformation of Ivorian popular music. Another example is the work of Manu Dibango, a professional musician of international expertise and renown, and a leading figure in Afro-jazz, as director of the Orchestre de la radiodiffusion télévision ivoirienne (Nyamnjoh 2020; Pajon 2021). This cultural melting pot had an influence on Ivorian music thanks to television, records and individual contacts with Ivorian figures (Mobio Agbakou Ludovic, Ernesto Djédjé, Mamadou Doumbia, Bailly Spinto, Yapi Amadékan, Aïcha Koné, Jeanne Agnimel, etc.) At the time (1978), 'it was see Abidjan or die', as Pierre 'Dizzy' Mandjeku put it. There was an artistic effervescence that touched every aspect of cultural life. It was reinforced by the opening of the JBZ studio in 1978, which was to stimulate Ivorian and West African production. It was no longer necessary to use RTI equipment or travel to Ghana, Nigeria or France to record music. *Highlife*, then *Afrobeat*, would no longer reign supreme. The effects of inter-cultural exchange were reinforced by the rapid globalisation of other styles such as *soul music* and *funk music*. While Accra was the capital of *highlife* and Lagos the capital of *afrobeat*, Abidjan was trying to position itself as the capital of *funk* and *disco* (Contreras 2016), the dance music par excellence. The JBZ studio, which was born at the heart of this explosion, was probably one of the first *world music* laboratories.

Since the 1970s, with the development of cities and the mass media, mass consumption and mass culture have developed. With mass consumption comes (paradoxically) a growing demand for authenticity. In the case of Côte d'Ivoire, the debate is particularly fierce because the colonial period has left traces that are slow to fade and wounds that are difficult to heal. Social life changed radically (see Vidal 1992; Ouattara 1985; Touré 1981). The movement continued over the next two decades. In the 1980s, with the globalisation of American music, young Ivorians 'responded' with Ivorian *country-folk* music, *hip hop*, *break dancing* and so on.

The city is a formidable melting pot where people, ideas and objects circulate, abound and mix. Obviously, Abidjan appears to be an obligatory stopover, a springboard for many musical artists waiting to conquer Europe and the rest of the world. Côte d'Ivoire has long been a haven for people, including artists fleeing dictatorial political regimes or political instability in neighbouring countries. On the one hand, Ivorian music lovers have proved receptive to *highlife*, Congolese *rumba*, *makossa* and many other African rhythms and genres. Côte d'Ivoire, and Abidjan in particular, has also played a role in the real flowering of artists. 'For West African musicians, Abidjan and Côte d'Ivoire are naturally a kind of launch pad, a hub from which their international careers can take off towards other horizons' (Ngoran 2013: 174).

The picture painted above is not the story of a smooth cultural melting pot. 'Culture' and 'politics' have a complex and conflicting relationship. This 'extrovert musicalisation' (Dédy 1984:119) of programming in the mass media and in performance venues is not to the taste of some Ivorian artists and intellectuals. Their music was disqualified and relegated to the rank of 'folklore' (Dédy 1984). Indeed, this opening up to the outside world was appreciated in different ways: some hailed the opening up to the world necessary for development (synonymous with civilisation), while others cried cultural alienation threatening traditional local cultures. But television is sorely lacking in programmes and is filling its schedule with programmes borrowed from Western television, mostly French, 'ready to broadcast', while benefiting from the aid of cooperation and development organisations and institutions. The result is a (remarkable) diversity of programmes in which music and, more generally, popular Ivorian 'culture' struggle to find a place. Paradoxically, the Ivorian mass media, while attempting to promote local realities and culture, tend to promote (more) the Americanised culture in the process of globalisation. National artists, rather on a 'popular commission', would mainly only perform in makeshift dance bars on the outskirts of the capital (Abobo, Yopougon, Port-Bouët, Treichville). Many musicians of the time saw this extraversion (openness) as a loss of earnings and a hindrance to the revival of national music, if not its liquidation.

In the cities, pioneer orchestras are often places of inter-ethnic and intercultural mixing. Many of the musicians and singers, former *sidemen* (musicians or choristers) in these pioneer orchestras, were undoubted schools of music. They in turn became leaders whose orchestral ensembles were laboratories for experimenting with blends and creating musical styles. Compared with the pre-colonial and colonial periods, 'the era of independence is above all one of interference and syncretism' (Wondji 1986a:22). Treichville was a place for mixing people and genres, people and cultures (Rouch 1959), the showcase of Abidjan as a world city (Vidal 2002).

Mass society is established, takes hold of cultural objects and gives birth to mass culture (Arendt 1972[2005]:265). In the 1980s, FM (frequency modulation) really penetrated Africa and improved listening quality (Tudesq 1999). Radio truly emerged as the *mass media* par excellence, particularly in its capacity for mass dissemination. The media, themselves 'generators of new ritual manifestations, specific to modern times' (Coman 2003:9), have the capacity to amplify public participation or the prestige of the artist or the 'hit'. Hence, popular song itself can be seen as mass communication.

The decade from 1975 to 1985 was a period of relative musical effervescence: each ethnic group (so to speak) 'modernised' its traditional music, translating it into the codes of a synthetic musicality underway in the public arena. This can be seen as the real beginning of Ivorian musical synthesis. The music was rejuvenated, 'intellectualised', and 'curiously' popularised. Despite the limited resources of a Côte d'Ivoire in the throes of a major economic crisis, there was hope of an improvement in living conditions and integration into the economic fabric.

Wondji (1986a) speaks of the development of music from all the regions of Côte d'Ivoire, which will have their own modern singers. In short, the culture disseminated by the *mass media* is becoming a consumer good, and the value of an artist tends to be gauged by the extent of his media coverage or his share of voice; the risk lies in the fact that the nature of these cultural objects can be altered as soon as they are 'modified – rewritten, condensed, digested, reduced to the state of junk for reproduction or image' (Arendt 1972[2005]:265), culture being destroyed in order to engender leisure.

The development of modern popular urban music in Côte d'Ivoire inevitably took place in the burgeoning city, the urbanisation and metropolisation of Abidjan (the country's economic capital). Abidjan was trying to compete with Kinshasa in terms of atmosphere, the good life – a world of resourcefulness in which, all things considered, social success was possible. Ivorian cities changed a great deal between the post-war years and the time of this study, over a period of seventy years (see Kipré, 1985, 1986, 1975). Abidjan is becoming a metropolis, or is in the midst of a process of metropolisation (Bassand 2001). Abidjan is undergoing major restructuring. It is characterised by its sprawl, 'encouraging the redeployment of social segregation and specialisation, even ghettoisation, in a kind of "systematic functional specialisation of the land" bringing together more or less homogenous types of activity in specific areas (i.e. business district, administrative district, shopping district, residential district, "dormitory" district, etc.)' (Bassand 2001:34). Phenomena of 'sub-urbanisation' and 'periubarnisation', emptying urban centres of the middle social classes, are developing at the same time as a kind of infra-urbanisation characterised by spontaneous informal housing on undeveloped sites (Bassand 2001:34). With metropolisation, a 'systematic disconnection between space and time is taking place, amplifying the fragmented lives of metropolitan dwellers'.

Metropolisation greatly accentuates individualism and individuation, while easing certain social constraints (Bassand 2001:37). The situation in which these musicians evolve and urban music develops is that of 'metropolity' (Bassand 2001:37). This neologism refers to the new forms and modes of sociability that are emerging and developing in metropolitan environments. They are characterised by the affirmation of individual autonomy. One of these new modes of sociability is 'networked sociality', the advantage of which is that it combines maximum connectivity and autonomy in a highly flexible way (Bassand 2001:37). This concept thus refers to the local and the global, two metropolitan horizons that are articulated in the concept of *glocal*. *Glocality* is therefore an important aspect of metropolity (Bassand 2001:38). Social and cultural diversity is seen as an asset rather than a threat, and this implies changes in the socialisation and integration of foreigners in the metropolis (Bassand 2001:38). In this configuration, particularly with courtyard housing, the neighbourhood becomes very important and is a player that tends to supplant the family.

As a social space for artistic practices, the city becomes the place for social practices of representation and cultural mediation. The city will become what we might call the natural space for the emergence and development of artistic activity, in other words, an activity of communication and representation that only has meaning and consistency if it is exercised in the public space. (Lamizet 2002:62)

The relationship between the global and the local, the rural and the urban, often leads to dead-ends – as repulsive points rather than poles of attraction. The 'glocal' thus seems to be more operative in the reality created by the globalisation movement. Rurbanity is linked to glocality in the same place, in the same rental location. In our view, the nuance between rurbanity and glocality is a question of scale. In such an ambiguous space, we postulate that the individual, the atom of action, does not live alone in the world, no longer lives alone in the world, but belongs to a network and therefore belongs to the glocal. However, in our view, the individual, or actor-network (Latour 2007), does not cancel out the individual's individuality and active role. Music is a perfect illustration of the malleability of the globalised world, in which distance does not cancel out the possibility of hybridisation, of appropriation of new sounds, of 'cross-fertilisation', and which 'makes all kinds of local appropriations and alterations possible, largely facilitated by a certain attenuation of the language barrier' (Bonniol 1999:321).

The newly independent state, despite its efforts to raise itself to the level of the most advanced peoples in the world, had difficulty satisfying the 'cultural needs' of its people. Popular song took on the task of filling this gap 'by expressing the aspirations of the popular masses for greater freedom, justice, solidarity and social progress. By promoting national languages and knowledge of the past, it testifies to the desire for cultural and linguistic resourcefulness that should enable the real achievement of national independence' (Wondji 1986a:21).

With 'the modernisation of orchestras and ... the contribution of foreign musical styles', Ivorian popular music experienced a real boom marked by 'interference and syncretism' (Wondji 1986a:22). There is constant communication between town and country, and in particular intense artistic communication. Town and country are no longer discriminating criteria. Moreover, the difference between rural popular music and urban popular music is becoming so tenuous that its heuristic (ontological) utility is questionable. 'The syncretism of themes, musical techniques and rhythms reveals the intensity of urban-rural exchanges, which contribute to the fragmentation of the spaces and audiences of [popular] song, and attest to the desire for cultural/artistic revival' (Wondji 1986a:22). But all popular singers (rural or urban) are subject to the laws of the market.

The structural adjustment plans of the 1980s, and the disastrous progress of the globalisation of economic liberalism, against a backdrop of weakening developmentalist and modernising ideologies, have laminated a fragile and relatively unstable Ivorian society. It is no longer the role of the weakened State to modernise the country and its people by combating 'traditions' that are synonymous with atavism, obscurantism, underdevelopment and so on. On the contrary, the state is going to encourage these 'traditions' and tend to 'heritage them as "regional" or "ethnic" components of a "national identity"' (Bazin 2014:17). 'Traditions' are no longer opposed to 'modernity', he explains. On the contrary, the latter (modernity) passes through 'traditions'. This certainly encourages the blending of these two diffuse 'entities'. This mix of traditional and modern music is expressed in places where musical groups once described as 'typical' perform regularly. Yopougon became a mecca for night-time festivities. In the early 1980s, Côte d'Ivoire was home to major public concerts in stadiums.

The rise of the *mass media* plays a very important role in the dissemination of popular culture. Popular culture is 'a space in movement whose centres of development evolve according to historical periods' (Mouchtouris 2007:42). In many respects, independent, post-colonial Côte d'Ivoire resembled a cultural crossroads where the Ivorians' own voice, or originality and musical specificity, was in short supply. This is also part of what, in all likelihood, forms the basis of the alibi for the quest for an identity of one's own: Ivoirité – which is at the same time a political struggle/revindication (Bahi 2013).

This period in Ivorian history saw a particular emphasis on the importance of 'development' – a veritable ideology that affected all sectors and 'compartments' of society: media for development, journalism for development, culture for development, starting with the education sector for development' (cf. the experience of school and out-of-school television). Reflections and debates on the loss of traditional values in favour of Western values, cultural alienation and cultural domination are lively and often corrosive, based on the (Marxist) principle that the culture of the dominant classes is (*de facto*) the dominant culture (cf. Touré 1981). Ivorian song, still embryonic and weak, seemed to have a compromised future, given that Ivorian youth were expected to lose their (traditional) culture because they were 'entirely under the yoke of American fashion in terms of music, dance, and sometimes even speech, in a word, the American way of life' (Ouattara 1985:84). These reflections on the alienation of the dominant culture, on the influence of African Americans on young Ivorians, in short on the development of the country that had gone astray in the form of westernisation, fit in with the myths, mythologies and contradictory developmentalist imaginary in which the period was immersed. In the mid 1980s, however, alongside this North American influence, Ivorian music was developing at its own pace, incorporating influences from all over.

Any individual or collective creation is 'permanently shaped by a collective expectation', and we can bet that musical artists know how to 'respond to a society's horizon of expectations by capturing in a work the latent but active myths of that society' (Walter 2011:44). However, in the face of well-founded fears and the real risk of losing this 'traditional' or 'authentic' Ivorian culture, something new came into being: the 1990s were to give rise to new and innovative musical genres (forms), synthetic and 'syncretic', such as *ziguéhi, zoblazo, zouglou, zogoda,* and so on, which were to be the first to be developed in the Ivorian music scene.

The 1990s saw the specialisation or 'thematisation' of the mass media, and the accentuation of musicalisation. They also saw a new effervescence brought about by the winds of liberalisation blowing around the world, at a time when pop culture and an American 'counter-culture' were being globalised, widely exploited, marketed and disseminated across the Atlantic. The role of the mass media in the rise of popular music is fundamental. Radio stations (private commercial radio stations, state radio stations, community radio stations) broadcast a lot of music because they were aimed at young audiences with an appetite for music, and their programmes were adapted to young people's tastes (Tudesq 2002:185–186). Ivorian television has also been won over by this musicalisation and is trying to maintain the memory of the music, dance and atmosphere of yesteryear – a past that is ultimately that of colonial times.

We are therefore also witnessing the emergence of 'another' trend. Local music is being translated into Western musical codes. Local rhythms are 'modernised' (reconstituted, reconfigured, reinterpreted) and reproduced with modern Western instruments. *Rock'n'roll* and *pop* music, on the other hand, are sung in local languages and even give rise to local styles. 'Urban culture differs from village culture in that the city is a place of mixing, contact, exchange, communication and intense cultural production that feeds off village agricultural surpluses' (Warnier 2007:20). This is so true that the city even exerts an attraction on people, young people in particular; an attraction that has become a social problem addressed by state propaganda (communication).

3 The *Musicscape* of the Multiparty Years

The globalisation of the flow of cultural goods favours the creation of popular music. The rise of modern popular music is first and foremost dependent on the network of maritime exchanges and communications on the Atlantic coast of Africa, part of the Euro-American world-system. Taken as a whole, modern popular music appears to be a 'melting pot of contextual and fluctuating identifications' (Warnier 2007:9). Thinking about modern popular music requires us to go beyond or abandon the category of ethnicity, of terr(it)oir(e) [of the limitation of the terroir and the delimitation of the territory], of the local (Appadurai 2001), of the petrified identity, presupposing a homogeneous, sumptuous [luxuriant] and independent (ethnic) culture, threatened with extinction [with disappearance] under the hegemonic (and 'culturophagous') effect of Western culture (or, in more contemporary terms, of globalisation).

By looking inside the 'spheres of interaction' or 'world systems' (Warnier 2007:23–24) of interconnected communities, we can understand how modern popular music has developed into the *musicscape of* today. A concept forged for the purposes of this study, the *musicscape* appears both as a component of the *soundscape* (Murray Schafer 1979[2010]) and as a sub-category of *mediascapes* (Appadurai 2001). However, it should not imply an idea of statism or obliterate the idea of 'circulation'. Rather, from now on it should be used to account for this (luxuriant) landscape of ever-mixing genres and styles, and to escape the gaping trap of musical ethnicity.

Côte d'Ivoire has willy-nilly embraced globalisation, of which the development of cities is one of the effects. The distinction between rural and urban is becoming even less clear-cut, but is still substantial. In many cases, the village remains the place of ontological identification and the first refuge. From this perspective, the Ivorian city, which has undergone an extraordinary transformation, is no longer a 'foreign cyst', 'an island of European modernity in a hostile environment' (Piermay 2003:45). It is undergoing continuous change, but this does not mean that it is losing its links with the village. On the contrary, complex relationships are being established between the rural and urban worlds, between the city and the village of origin, and in this in-between area, people are 'developing complex strategies to make the most of various opportunities' (Piermay 2003:40). The city is therefore no longer seen as a predator or destroyer of African society, but as one of the places where it is constructed, in short from the point of view of the significant role it plays in the (re)production of society [of the social] (Piermay 2003:35). The (African) city is a lush environment, and its actors reflect its changes, challenges and diversity (Piermay 2003:40): 'Formal and informal, modernity and heritage, Western technology and witchcraft, etc., all play a complex role in the construction of the African city' (Piermay 2003:42). Despite all kinds of difficulties, the city remains a place of contact and exchange: a place of hybridisation, ingenuity and invention – a place of creation (creativity), where the unprecedented (the new, the unexpected) and the unusual (the bizarre, the baroque) emerge. The very creation of music is linked to the city: 'Music depends on the city, its moods and its scenes of life; it is like a second life of the city; it captures and interprets the whims, trends, fashions and customs that develop in the city, translating them into its own language' (Gondola 2003:112).

The musical milieu is seen as one of these teeming fields, and music is part of these bricolages, these links and these opportunities in a city that is seen here 'in terms of invention, that is to say, of unexpected and baroque assemblages that make it possible to provide a response to the innumerable problems encountered' (Piermay 2003:45). The unexpected developed in this teeming environment. The modernisation sought by the fathers of independence accelerated, bringing with it industrialisation, cultural industries, and a distinction between cultivated culture and popular culture (Caune 1995), opposing a westernised, 'modern' culture on the one hand and a 'traditional' African culture on the other, determining the manufacture and market of cultural products. The rise of the mass media has led to the popularisation and massification of music. The trend towards the musicalisation of radio has been accentuated by the specialisation of this medium. This musicalisation has also taken hold on television, which has also been affected by the beginnings of 'thematisation', while being reinforced by dance and music videos. Music is now seen as a commodity, viewed from a marketing perspective with hyperspecialised agents embedded in a complex (commercial) economic system.

With the reintroduction of a multiparty system in 1990, the freedom of speech also liberated popular song. The 'galère', the horizontality of misery, was no longer hidden away, but sung and broadcast over the airwaves. *Zouglou was* born of a synthesis of local rhythms, while taking up the traditional singer's role as truth-teller, conscientious objector, ideological and moral sentinel of society.

The aspirations and needs of these young people have exploded – increased – in the space of two generations. The liberalisation brought about by the introduction of a multi-party system and the development of the media have, in theory, made it possible for young people to express themselves. For all that, the habits inherited from three decades of a single party did not suddenly change. This decade, the dawn of the third millennium, also saw the emergence of a consumer society and major political tensions. The combined effects of the (neo)liberal economic option and democratisation are reflected in the current diversity of music in Côte d'Ivoire. Modern urban popular music is developing and becoming more democratic. Modern popular music is increasingly asserting itself as a media form – as a medium understood here in a broad sense (Weaver 1949:95), fulfilling the same functions as other, more 'classical' urban media.

The 2000s were certainly the years when *zouglou* exploded onto the national scene. At the same time, criticism became more open, protest became more explicit and grumbling became more thunderous. *Zouglou was not the* only music to speak out. Reggae preceded it, albeit in a more allusive tone, by taking the liberty of questioning political leaders about the political drift of Ivorian politics. Popular music has been marked by the Ivorian crisis, particularly the paroxysmal one that erupted in September 2002 (Bahi 2011). More than ever, the figure of the popular singer as political flagship is taking shape.

Meanwhile, the *Disc Jockey* (DJ) phenomenon, made possible by the combined effect of advances in music technology, the spread of the internet and globalisation, is spreading throughout Côte d'Ivoire among musicians and technicians. Ivorian DJs, also following the global movement and spreading to Côte d'Ivoire, are leaving the maquis or *nightclubs* they used to run to make their own albums (audio phonic cassettes and compact discs) and give shows and live concerts, thus becoming artists in their own right, veritable *show business* stars.

The 2000s also saw the explosion of the coupé décalé phenomenon which, like disco, is dance music for fun, where the only thing that counts is the '*show*', the 'atmosphere', the hedonism, the 'racket', and so on (Kolé 2023). He seems to be deliberately turning his back on a 'tradition' of Ivorian (or even African) singers that seems to have its origins in traditional music, leaving aside the function of 'ideological and moral sentinel' (Wondji 1986b), and does not consider consciousness-raising to be important. Music is no longer intentionally a medium for delivering educational, moralising and other messages.

Many musical genres are doomed to an ephemeral existence. Against all the odds, *coupé décalé* seems to be settling in, forming with *reggae* and *zouglou* the troika of modern Ivorian popular music. *Coupé décalé* even completes the affirmation of a young music and (sub)culture. The deaths of its messianic figures – Douk Saga, the founder, and DJ Arafat, the emblematic figure – were presented by the media and experienced by many young people as national mourning.

'Rurbanity' and 'glocality', because they combine to give rise to new cultural forms and practices, are at the beginning and the end of the phenomenality of modern popular music. Modern popular music radiates with the unfolding urban space and the changing world of mixing and exchange. It does not develop in a vacuum, but according to a principle of cultural and political transformation that includes circulatory movements of people, ideas and objects between African and American creative centres (Feld 1988) and, more broadly, from Africa to the (rest of) the world via its diaspora and vice versa (Zeleza 2005: 220; Gilroy 2010; Martin 2012).

During the single party era, the *mass media* (notably radio and television) played a decisive role in promoting Ivorian music. As part of their public service remit, they programmed musicians from all regions of the country, out of a concern for regional cultural balance and respect for Côte d'Ivoire's cultural diversity. They have been able to serve as a launch pad for young talents such as Alpha Blondy.

As a living art form, music appealed to audiences because it met their aspirations and expectations, but also and above all because of its ability 'to draw on local or regional heritage, integrating external contributions including those of colonisation, and indebted to 'imagination, rural exodus and the influences of international media' (Doua 2009:6). This is what terms such as 'tradi-moderne' or 'afropop' refer to. The latter sometimes refers to contemporary African popular music, or African pop. It is characterised by a fusion of American and African popular music, sounds and dances. The artist-musician Meiway is a perfect illustration of this. But in reality, these names hide a major difficulty in characterising musical genres and styles. Pablo de Gokra, for example, follows in the footsteps of Amédée Pierre, who in turn follows in the footsteps of the 'traditional' singer *tohourou*.

If we go back as far as possible in the history of Côte d'Ivoire, we can see that the development (expansion, amplification, growth) of modern popular music (including urban music) was made possible by maritime trade in the context of urban development. The COVID-19 pandemic demonstrated the weaknesses (vulnerability) of sub-Saharan African cities, with their somewhat chaotic urbanisation, uneven infrastructure and lush informal settlements. But this period was also a good one for music on the Internet, as demonstrated by the *Jerusalema* phenomenon that has conquered the planet. Modern popular music is therefore emerging from a lush urban culture, while at the same time being dependent on technological inventions and innovations in the world of music itself, and in the mass media and (tele)communications in general. Its industrial production and distribution is amplified by the effects of globalisation. Marketing segmentations – such as *world music*, 'urban music', etc. – do not seem to be very productive for grasping the abundance and complexity of modern popular music.

The analysis of popular music generally remains dependent on a very fixed approach to the largely dominant colonial reality. Colonialism itself caricatured the differences and reinforced the borders (initially physical when it did not create them) between peoples in the imagination. But the cultural links between peoples have not changed as a result of this caricatured structuring of differences between peoples. The conditions for the deployment of modern popular music are captured in the pairs of tensions local/global and urban/rural, which are subsumed in the glocal/rural pair. We need to take account of the consequences of globalisation, including democratisation, the opening up of societies, their trans-locality and so on. The current *musicscape* is therefore the result of interactions (between) town and country, and not of a rupture between the two, but of a labile and productive rurbanity on the one hand. At the same time, on a (much) more macro scale, it is the product of the global/local tension, whose respective feedback loops produce effects on both the local and the global, and which the neologism 'glocal' attempts to capture.

Before analysing popular music as an act of cultural mediation, it is important to analyse the forms and acts of communication (mediation) that occur within it, and to pay particular attention to the processes of identification and social belonging that are at work. But first, it seems desirable and necessary to enter the world of Ivorian music, to infiltrate the places and figures of its production in order to understand how this medium functions.

4 Poietics of Musical Art in Abidjan

This chapter examines the 'making' (or 'creation') of music by 'young' musicians aspiring to stardom on the basis of in situ observations in performance venues (recording studios). Drawing firmly on the work of Jean-Pierre Warnier (2007) and Victor Turner (1988, 1969[1997]), it follows as far as possible the lineaments of the poietics or fabrication of popular music in order to grasp the springs of originality and/or authenticity. The topical object of poietics in art is strictly the study of the process of creating the work: 'Poietics is less concerned with the artist's affects than with the dynamic lineaments, voluntary or involuntary, that link him to the work in progress. In short, its object is the *poiesis* that confronts the creator with his project, and not the *aisthesis* that he may experience in his action, or arouse by it' (Passeron 1999:269–270).

Creative behaviour presupposes the acquisition of knowledge and know-how, and requires the investment of physical space and the use of devices and technical and technological artefacts. The aim of the poietic study is therefore first and foremost to identify the 'techniques', the 'poietic strategies' that have guided the making of the work (Molino 2009; Nattiez 2009) and to identify the compositional 'ideas', the harmonic structures (the chords), the tools (instruments, digital interfaces, computer, etc.), the work in rehearsal, in the studio, and so on. In short, it is a question of keeping track of the 'techniques', the 'poietic strategies' that have guided the making of the work (Molino 2009; Nattiez 2009). In short, it's a question of taking into account 'everything that was important (material, technical, procedural, relational, communicational, somatic, mental, imaginary, fantastical, etc.) for the creator(s) at the moment of creating the work' (Forest 2013:12). In short, we are talking about a whole range of elements that are necessary for musical practices and the making of modern popular music, and which condition the skills and performances (performativity) of the creative process and creation itself. Whatever the type of artistic practice, poietics is understood as 'an experiential approach to the dynamic processes at work in the creation of a work' (Paillé 2004:11). Poietics therefore refers us to a kind of anthropology of creation – of artistic production – that focuses more on the relationship between the artist and his work than on the artist himself, in his creative space (studio, rehearsal room, etc.) and his experience of this (these) space(s) (Goffman 1991). This requires the researcher (i) to take an interest in the acquisition of artistic and musical knowledge (and know-how), that is, in training, and (ii) to enter the music-making workshop, because 'in truth the place of art is first and foremost the workshop' (Passeron 1999:274).

Another aspect of the history and transformation of modern popular music in Côte d'Ivoire is thus outlined. The historicisation of amplified popular music is a difficult undertaking because, in addition to the lack of reliable sources, it is undermined by the (marketing) cleavages of genres, the journalistic expertise of music critics, the territorial divisions of academic research and interdisciplinary 'competition' (Gibert & Leguern 2008). Indeed, 'the workshop, studio or mixing room are places that are as physical as they are mental, material as they are experiential, technical as they are aesthetic' (Forest 2013:9). These contemporary creators of popular music are attentive to their popular African heritage. They create with a compositional ethos that values, respects and even venerates this heritage. While admitting foreign influences, the quest for originality does not radically change this heritage (Agawu 2016:206, 295).

Making music also requires equipment and infrastructure. The Ivorian music scene is characterised by a lack of musical infrastructure and a shortage of musical instruments and accessories. Many musicians, apart from the fact that they have few financial resources, are faced with questions that are difficult to resolve: where can they find guitar strings, bass strings, drumsticks, drum heads, and other parts at reasonable prices? Where and how can you get good instruments (well-made and fair) at a good price? Apart from Catholic or evangelical churches, and the rare orchestras that are subsidised or financed by patrons, and which make instruments of various qualities available to musicians, it's a case of finding your own way – and that starts with training.

Bergson (1936) thought that the artist is capable of perceiving, and in a way translating, what the *vulgum pecus* cannot always grasp. In the Bété worldview (for example), precociousness is perfectly understandable, because art, and music in particular, is considered to be a gift and is innate; it runs in the family, so to speak, and the artist is predestined (Séry 2015:53, 102). But the artist's technical training, whether inherited or received from a master, remains important and necessary. This is how the 'traditional' griot has survived the centuries and adapted to social change (Niane 1960; Laye

1978; Sadji 1985; Cissé & Kamissoko 1988; Camara 1992). The *djuésrofouè*[1] rhapsode baoulé (Tonton Etienno), the aède sénoufo (Zélé de Papara) or even the *tohourou*[2] chansonnier bété, often presented as 'traditional', are in fact relatively recent inventions (Hobsbawm 2006[2012]) – that is, from the colonial period. These recently developed 'traditions' now seem centuries old, producing an effect of myth and false continuity with the past, when in reality they are more akin to dissidence from that past.

The Baule chansonnier uses (or even makes) his *kpaniglo*, a tetrachord guitar imitated from the Western guitar – itself introduced into Africa by the Portuguese probably in the fifteenth century and fairly widespread in French West Africa towards the end of the nineteenth century (among others by *Krus* sailors). The first guitars and phonographs were introduced in Côte d'Ivoire at the beginning of the twentieth century: phonographs in particular were intro-duced between 1930 and 1940, and guitars from the 1940s onwards (Mazzoleni 2010). In this way, something new was created, like the naïfs (in the visual arts) inspired by this traditional world that changed so abruptly with colonisation, rather like the movie *Les maîtres fous* (*The Mad Masters*) (Rouch 1955) who, through this representation, reflected the new 'civilisation' that was taking hold.

The heritage is identifiable in the musical (poietic) work itself. The musical poietic process is linked to the musician's training (initial and ongoing). Training (initial and ongoing), by transmitting the musician's own musical *technique* and practice, contingent on his imagination and creative capacities, determines [limits or liberates, restricts or extends] his poietic work. Here, orality and various modes of learning rub shoulders and intermingle (Diawara 2015).

The apprentice musician has to face various obstacles before entering the world of music. Among the first means and places of musical training and apprentice-ship are certainly the brass bands or military band orchestras. Local brass bands were probably among the first attempts to translate African music into Western musical codes, Western harmony and Western tempered instruments (Dagri 2019a). At the very beginning of the 1960s, the Régie Abidjan-Niger (RAN) music school attended by the children of expatriates and those of the local bourgeoisie had a certain importance in the musical training of Ivorians (Goran 2011; Ouattara & Lasme 2016; Kanga & Goran 2017). The National Arts Institute (INA), created in 1965, took over musical training (especially classical). Later, it was to play a certain role in Ivorian musical production, particularly in the translation of local music, as well as in the consumption of this music.

However, its impact on the development of music in Côte d'Ivoire remained limited for a long time, insofar as the secondary school music teachers trained in

---

[1] *Djuésrofouè* lit. 'the one who sings' ...   [2] *Tohourou* litt. 'give him advice' ...

classical music by this establishment were transferred to schools and had few resources or opportunities for instrumental practice. They were content mainly with theoretical lessons, the results of which had little effect on their pupils' schooling. The creation of an (African?) musicology department at the Institut national des arts (INA) in 1984 made it possible to train music education teachers (rather than musicians) for teaching in state schools. Indeed, music education is that 'discipline which deals, on the one hand, with the teaching and learning of music and, on the other, with education in the social and cultural aspects of the sound code and noises in our world today' (Kanga & Goran 2017:49).

Apart from modern music schools and conservatoires, many musicians often learn music 'on the job', intuitively, in an oral tradition where imitation reigns supreme (Titon 1992:168). For those who have the means, the Internet, particularly through educational capsules, is playing an increasingly important role in training. In an amateur-style apprenticeship (Flichy 2010), they can acquire a few rudiments of organology, elements of theory, musical practice and a degree of technical skill or even virtuosity. These young musicians, 'neophytes' in a liminal phase (Van Gennep 1909[1981]:14, 27), are on the threshold of the musical field, in a situation of profane 'liminality' (Turner 1969[1997]:96–97) and, as 'liminal entities', are subject, if not to the authority of the community, at least to that of a mentor. This means that musical training, both theoretical and practical, is often rudimentary or even non-existent if we consider the music school institution. Self-taught, then, learning on the job, knowing at best how to follow a 'grid', their real school is made up of listening to the genres and successes of their favourite musicians, 'tips' [or *'topos'* or *'plans'*] taken from professional musicians, or musicians they consider more advanced than themselves.

Musical training was often acquired on the job 'in the street' from another DIY enthusiast. 'The bricoleur addresses a collection of residues of human works, in other words, a subset of culture' (Lévi-Strauss 1962:29). As for the artist, 'he is both a scholar and a bricoleur' (Lévi-Strauss 1962, 33). This bricolage is not specific to Côte d'Ivoire or to Ivorian musicians. Rather, it seems to us to be a worldwide or globalised phenomenon that in truth reflects amateurism, if not on the increase, at least more visible and triumphant, facilitated by the democratisation of technology (Flichy 2010). One of the consequences of their limited musical training is that these musicians have a restricted and relatively closed (inward-looking) harmonic and melodic universe. This did not prevent virtuosos from appearing in their ranks. During this liminal period, a spirit of friendship developed between them. The fact that they sometimes frequent the same places of worship reinforces the spirit of camaraderie and confraternity as a prelude to full entry into the musical field and full participation in the community of musicians.

Music is one of those arts that you learn as you practice. There are many different places to learn, including all the places where the initiator and the initiate can put themselves in a learning situation. These spaces range from the private sphere (the bedroom) to rehearsal rooms (private paying rooms, churches, private homes, improvised spaces), recording studios and young musical groups. These youth music groups function like groups ('small groups') of young people or teams of artists (in this case budding artists) and, as such, are 'microscopic shelters', cemented together by music, where the individual, the young neophyte musician, as an individual, will play out (or commit) his or her life.

The modern folk music in question here is fundamentally unwritten. It is an oral tradition on at least two levels: (i) at the level of sources of inspiration, ancient unwritten 'folk' music (Zadi 1977); (ii) at the level of learning 'by word of mouth', by direct imitation; (iii) at the level of performance or interpretation of musical pieces, where the ear and memory – reproduction *a memoria* – play a key role. They can then develop an expertise in the genres and stars they adore and imitate. Since the elements collected and used by DIY artists are 'pre-stressed' (Lévi-Strauss 1962:29) and their possibilities (harmonic or even instrumental) are limited, (successful) transgression is always a sign, if not of innovation, at least of originality and the signal of a fashion, however ephemeral. Given their musical training, these singing musicians often have a DIY approach. Here the term 'bricolage' is used both from a theoretical (solfeggio, music theory, harmony, organology, music history, etc.) and a practical (instrumental practice and technique) point of view to describe these musically 'illiterate' artists – when they are not illiterate in the literal sense (Séry 2015). They make do with what they have, 'getting by' as they put it themselves.

The development of modern popular music in Côte d'Ivoire also depends on 'religious' music. Of course, the INA and then the INSAAC (Institut national supérieur des arts et de l'action culturelle) trained many musicians for secondary schools and churches. But we must also take into account the important role played by the churches (Catholic, Protestant, Harrist, Evangelical, Pentecostal) themselves, particularly in instrumental practice, as well as in choral singing and choir training. Personal initiatives (individual or collective) by music teachers also play a part in this musical training. Until relatively recently, the (Catholic) Church extolled the beauty of liturgical chant, which was necessarily Western. It decried African worship practices and disparaged local cultural values. It was after the Second Vatican Council (1965) that 'religious' (Catholic) music became Africanised with the arrival of drums and clicks. Pressed onto CDs, it will be added to secular music – music for secular use – even if God is being sung. For many musicians, those looking for an outlet other than that of 'college music teacher', church services, 'crusades' and evangelisation campaigns serve to play for God ('to give thanks') but are also opportunities to 'perform' .

It's difficult to learn music without making it. Making music presupposes performance, and presupposes the ideas of realisation and behaviour (conduct): it is the (concrete) implementation of (technico-)musical (and 'para-musical') competence in the production of musical statements. This performance, as an act of communication and/or accomplishment (Bauman 1992:44), is most evident in rehearsal and performance or spectacle (Schechner 2008, 1985; Béhague 1992:177). Self-education plays an important role in the itineraries of young musicians.

5 Tribality and Network Logic

Musical poetics necessarily involves 'making music' (Schütz 2007; Agawu 2016:4), and ideally presupposes a grasp, through social relations and anthropo-logics (Balandier 1974[1985]), of the relationships of 'syntony' but also of tension and negotiation in the activities that, performed together by the actors in space and time, are at the heart of the creative process. We are in the middle of 'musical communication', in the heart of the machinery and the making of popular music. So we can understand how popular music is made as an art form, and grasp the role of technology in the creative process by starting to understand how it is transmit-ted. Music is one of those ephemeral material forms whose mode of transmission is oral and relies primarily on memory (auditory and visual) even if, in reality, 'different modes of cultural transmission adapt to different forms of legitimation' (Rowlands 1993:150). It is here that secrecy and ambiguity, whether intended or not by the master who delivers his teaching, creep in.

Indeed, (musical) art, as the product of collective action, requires its agents to collaborate in the creation of works. This collaboration is possible because the agents share common presuppositions, conventions and so on. When such cooperation occurs repeatedly and even habitually between the same individ-uals, or individuals who are sufficiently similar to be considered identical, we can speak of the existence of 'an art world' (Becker 1988[2006]:99). The expression art world refers to 'the network of all those whose activities, coordinated through a common knowledge of conventional means of work, contribute to the production of the very works that make the art world famous' (Becker 1988[2006]:22). In practice, the makers and users of these works 'have mutually adapted their practices, so that the organisation of production and use remains, for a time, a stable unit, a *world*' (Becker 2009:22). Understanding the making of music therefore involves analysing the organ-isational aspects, processes, logics, norms and values, recipients, networks, alliances and conflicts, and imaginary worlds at work in this specific world of musical art (Becker 2009:22–30).

Intuitive marketing based on a certain idea of public tastes and expectations also guides the manufacture of 'products'. The 'Ivorian' art world, made up of identifiable sub-groups, *'tribes'*, micro-groups, communities of emotion endowed with ethics and aesthetics, and which are part of a neo-tribalism 'characterised by fluidity, occasional gatherings, scattering' (Maffesoli 1988:116). This tribality – *reggae, zouglou, Rn'B-jazz, rap, coupé décalé,* etc. – conceals the idea of 'tribal art' and more or less implies (at the cost of a great simplification) 'a relationship between the social, the aesthetic and the temporal'. Admittedly, the identity dimensions of individuals and communities are complex and contrasting. There are 'continuities and values of artists in a given locality between arts of different periods and media'. (Picton 1992:28). We can ask with W. Fagg (quoted by Picton): 'how does this or that configuration of form relate to this or that social grouping in this or that temporal framework?' Heuristically, each '(neo-)tribe' has or constructs its own artistic universe (including dance, clothing, but also body art, graphic and pictorial arts, etc. – in short, an ethos and an aesthetic). However, despite this 'tribality', there are one or more links between these sub-cultures and a certain mobility (of musicians and technicians) is at work in this teeming milieu. In this world of resourcefulness, where survival is paramount, interactions between individuals (musicians, arrangers, producers, etc.) form links, connections, networks that are never definitive, but always in flux.

Abidjan favours the mixing of popular and cultural musical genres and forms. As a result of the very settlement of the city, whether by rural dwellers or nationals of other colonies, certain neighbourhoods became places of relocation during the colonial period (Balandier 1985, 1957; Rouch 1967, 1959). This trend continued and was accentuated later with the rural exodus and immigration. This new situation demystifies and renders obsolete the physical and spatially limited geographical notion of *'home'*, of terroir – *ipso facto* widening the question of citizenship, ethnic belonging, social ties, even the social and national imaginary, the nation – Abidjan thus becomes *"a home away from home"* for Syrian-Lebanese, Senegalese, French, Burkinabe, Nigerians, Cameroonians, and so on.

The Bété *tohourou* or the Baoulé chansonnier are modern musicians – an endogenous modernity. It is this modernity (or modernisation) that the somewhat 'essentialist' notion of 'tradi-moderne' (Kua-Nzambi Toko 2018) seeks to capture by presupposing that traditional and modern are fixed (or even pure) entities. Traditional music is neither anchored in a cultural latency, nor frozen in a traditional customary pastism, paralysed by its mode of conservation and transmission. Traditional music is part of 'culture-translation'. But this is not 'the identical reproduction of a set of fixed habits' (Warnier 2007:12). And more: 'In the fields of music, oral and written literature, bodily techniques, the arts and religious practices, individuals and groups are constantly inventing, innovating and renewing the cultural achievements of their society. No culture, no society, remains alive without engaging in ongoing cultural creation' (Warnier 2007:52–53).

In reality, this creative approach aims to (re)revive the artistic and musical heritage by covering, recycling and remixing traditional music in order to modernise it. This whole idea is a form of cannibalism (Nyamnjoh 2018), as Diawara (2015) also makes us understand in village musical poetics (in Mali). The production of remixes in the artistic world of modern popular music resonates with this (re-conceptualised) cannibalism.

This idea of the tribe fits in well with that of the construction of a collective identity and the social imaginary, even if it tends to overstate the case. The social imaginary can be conceived as 'all the imagined forms and contents that are part of social expressions and practices'.[3] In Durkheim's view, society is first and foremost constituted by 'the idea it has of itself', that is, by the autonomous collective representations that circulate in social life and weave the fabric of community consciousness: 'a whole world of feelings, ideas and images which, once born, obey laws of their own' (Durkheim 1912[2007]: 594–596). The social (and even national) imaginary of a country can no longer be conceived as being confined within geographical boundaries. More than ever, we must consider that African music in general, and Ivorian music in particular, develops within 'transnational cultural flows' (Appadurai 2001:90).

The (non-exhaustive) 'tribalisation' sketched out earlier refers to imaginary worlds nourished, among other things, by myths that serve to organise daily life and determine artistic creation. Here, passions, elective affinities and sectarian behaviour are important for actors inhabited by ideologies, collective representations and 'community' or 'subcultural' logics (Tacussel & Renard 1998:275–276). The language used in popular music is a mark of identity affirmation. Popular song often uses *Nouchi*, a variety of African French, the result of local appropriation of the language of the coloniser, which has become the language of power. This language can be conceived as an agent of instrumental, registral and above all identity-based legitimacy (Robillard quoted by Zang Zang 2018:7). It can also be understood, from a globalist perspective, as a contemporary crossbred language of other young languages, hybrid languages of African metropolises (Hindoubill, Camfranglais, Franfulfuldé, etc.), characterised by a mixture of codes (Boutin & Kouadio 2015:252) and which are part of the periphery of the global continuum of French (Zang Zang 2018:12).

More prosaically, it is the language of the street, often used by young people (whether or not they come from the street). In the absence of an 'Indigenous'

---

[3] Dictionnaire de sociologie Robert/Seuil (1999:270).

lingua franca, it is a place where the social imagination is created and a powerful site for composing and recognising a sense of community belonging, even if it's in a playful register. Used in popular song, it expresses in the most imaginative way what is perceived as coarse or vulgar in standard language. Language, the condition of normative and creative subjectivity, is the foundation of authenticity and subjection, and determines the 'capacity to act on the world'. Popular language, as a transgression of the official language and insubordination to the French language, is also the quest for the authentic.

The imaginary is a world of images, symbols and myths (Barthes 1957) that are autonomous but constitute a self-organised whole capable of rendering meaningful and creative 'the raw data of memory or perception'. It can be conceived as a network in which the different elements take on meaning in relation to each other: 'an immaterial bridge, but at the same time a very real one, insofar as it gives us the very real power of these images, unintelligible as long as they remain fragmentary' (Thomas 1998:16–17) through which man gives himself to see the world, and puts himself in touch with the world.

The question of the emergence (and existence) of a national music haunted the three decades of single-party rule: 'The more they felt that music was essential to the influence of peoples, the more they felt that the population was lagging behind nationally in this area' (Konaté 2002:777). National musicians internationalising local genres, artists acclimatising genres from elsewhere, did not resolve the question of national music, did not manage to become 'singers of Ivorian music' or national emblems. Armed with the pidginised French of the street, *zouglou* would undoubtedly sidestep the conscious or unconscious 'ethno-strategy' at work in the development of Ivorian music and position itself as national music (Konaté 2002:778). As for 'ethno-strategy' (Konaté 2002), it should be noted that music can be 'ethnic' and have a national (or even international) audience. The impact of the lyrics will certainly not be the same. Popular music also reveals an ethos (in the sense of a set of values, but also a lifestyle and a sense of achievement). It produces and reproduces a collective imagery (a set of images from the same origin) that is produced (reproduced), proposing a way of perceiving the world and of perceiving oneself in that world.

Music is also part of the construction of the collective identity of a group, a people, a human community. 'Identity is a more sociological concept than the ego, and one that is more difficult to grasp because it does not manifest itself directly in the behaviour of individuals. Identity is also a mechanism, a process, and processes are never directly observable' (Moessinger 2000:91). In Côte d'Ivoire, popular music is often reduced to *zouglou* or *reggae*, or even *coupé décalé*. Because of their hegemonic nature, they create a halo around modern popular music, which can now be seen as a sign of young people asserting their identity through insubordination to adult authority (Akindès 2002:101). Identity is often understood as having two dimensions: unity, which refers to 'a set of individual properties that remains relatively constant', and uniqueness, which refers to 'the specificity of the individual, to what makes him different from others, and most often refers to experience and subjectivity' (Moessinger 2000:95).

Popular music (in the sense of committed or non-committed popular music) constructs the uniqueness of the Ivorian as a collective feeling vis-à-vis a 'community self' and vis-à-vis others. In order to make a 'hermeneutic' of it, to draw out its meaning, we posit that this popular music participates in the process of constructing a collective Ivorian identity. In other words, the aim of this work is to understand popular music as language and communication. Understanding popular music as a form of social communication means interpreting its meaning, in other words, reconstructing the motives of social actors (Boudon 2003). Values such as 'hospitality' and 'pacifism' make up the representations of the stereotypical positive Ivorian identity, 'Ivorian-ness'. The symbolic aspect of a social fact is undoubtedly one of its properties (Mauss 1925[2012]). These highly symbolic values sketch out the imagined features of Côte d'Ivoire and the Ivorian. 'There *never was that, there isn't that and there never will be that'*. In this refrain from Pat Sacko's dream, *'that'* is used for 'Ivorians killing each other'.

Popular music, which internalises the values inseparable from the dominant ideology, is, as an expression of cultural identity, the verbalisation of a collective ego or superego (Fougeyrollas 1987:48–51). The musical expressions of young people bear witness to 'the conjunction between the uncertainty of the future elites and the disillusionment of those excluded from the system', out of step with an outdated discourse that has little credibility for these young people (Konaté 2002:778–779). Notwithstanding this, popular music, taken as a whole, conveys a sense of community, collective dreams.

The postulate here is a major one: the imaginary plays an important role in the establishment of a community (Castoriadis 1975; Anderson 1983). It therefore seems conceivable and even possible to understand (the worlds of) music through empirically identifiable 'tribes', 'communities', 'natural categorisations' and even subcultures. For example, we can broadly identify 'tribal' groups: *zouglou*, *youssoumba, coupé décalé*, and so on, and their successors . . . in short, those who perform at the Abidjan Urban Music Festival (*FEMUA*), but not exclusively. They have more or less marked and differentiated dress and language codes, greeting rituals, lifestyles (more community-based for the *rastas*), imaginary worlds, and so on and often have more or less dedicated social and performance spaces (cafés, maquis, bars, etc.), urban bubbles such as the street, the neighbourhood, the 'periphery', the university halls of residence, and so on. These groups form communities of sorts. All this seems to have the ingredients of tribality. These 'communities' are symptomatic of a 'tribalism' or even a 'neotribalism characterised by fluidity, occasional gatherings and scattering' (Maffesoli 1988:116) at the heart of the way popular music works. These tribal communities, far from being watertight, are characterised by a certain mobility, even nomadism, particularly among musicians who move from one tribe to another, which is a guarantee of creativity and innovation. Popular music is in fact conceived in terms of the 'hybridisation' and fusion made possible by the circulation of cultural and artistic products.

Cultural creativity is not limited to the national territory, but rather extends to a crossbreeding of belonging. The production or manufacture of Ivorian music (like much music) is a delocalised activity (Giddens 1994), we might even say deterritorialised or multi-territorial. Creation may well begin in Abidjan in one studio and be finalised elsewhere in another studio in another country in a diasporic environment, these *homes away from homes* which, despite their conscious or unconscious resistance, are themselves in the midst of a process of cultural 'hybridisation'. The African diaspora, which is extremely complex, plays a considerable role in the deterritorialised production of 'African' music in general (Nyamnjoh & Fokwang 2005:257).

It is together that the black diasporas specifically produce 'Ivorian' music. In Côte d'Ivoire itself, contacts and exchanges between musicians from other parts of Africa (Malians, Guineans, Ghanaians, Cameroonians, Liberians, Congolese – to give just a few examples), in certain districts of Abidjan (Marcory, Remblais, Yopougon, Abobo among others), encouraged creativity and musical creation, while at the same time influencing the construction of the social imagination. Zairean refugee musicians (fleeing economic hardship and then war in their own countries, waiting to return home or go to *Matongué* in Brussels) have had a considerable influence on DJ music. The formal analogy between *Ndombolo* (Biaya 2000) and the dances and atmosphere created by the DJs is striking.

Many of the young artists and listeners, often born in the city, have a floating relationship with the rural world, the terroir (Bahi 2010). This low attendance rate is usually explained by fear of witchcraft, reduced financial resources as a result of the economic situation (with the economic crisis, travelling to the village is expensive, especially if the village is far from Abidjan), and other factors. The fact remains that urban and rural boundaries are porous: towns and the hinterland are interconnected. The members of a family, whether they live in the city or the country, are interdependent, even creating a continuity. This continuity is conducive to artistic creation. Ultimately, for these young city dwellers, the village is really the neighbourhood (the *gbata*).

From the end of the 1970s onwards, a cultural and artistic ferment took place, characterised by the blending of the artistic sensibilities of Ivorians and artists of different origins, who had immigrated for various reasons to these places, which were ultimately places of cultural diversity, like hives of artists. This ferment has breathed new vitality into Ivorian popular music. New musical genres and styles are born from and within this socio-cultural effervescence. It's as if veritable youth subcultures have grown up around these musical styles. The differences between these styles are quite remarkable, even if the sedimentation is not 'solid' or rigid. Some young people wander from one style to another. This stylistic coasting is particularly true of musicians with a very good technical level who are capable of playing very different styles. These different musical genres and styles often share the same 'sharks' – musicians, technicians or arrangers. As a result, there are no watertight barriers between these musical genres, and there is always scope for mixing and mingling, and therefore for the unexpected.

Hybridisation and fusion have been joined by fusion. Emotional communities are expressed in the common phrase '*we're together*' ('*we do everything together*' and, more tragically, '*we die together*' in the post-election crisis of 2010). It's the idea of being together, this sociality that is revealed in essentially behavioural cultural elements: modes of dress, hairstyles, dance, gait, language, and which subsumes itself in 'style'. Clothes, hairstyles and accessories construct this 'good' or 'bad' taste, this look, this 'style', displayed in front of others as signs of recognition. Indeed, the body speaks: 'It bears the inscriptions, marks and attributes that express belonging, social identity and status. Clothing and bodily ornaments contribute to this definition, and gestures even more so' (Balandier 2008:59). All this contributes to the formation of urban subcultures shared by artists and their fans. They also act as beacons to which young people in need of reference points can relate. This form of identification, based on appearances and somewhat haphazard, nonetheless raises the question of what these 'tribes' have in common.

It could be argued that there is no such thing as an audience for popular song, given its great heterogeneity and the plasticity of Ivorian identity and popular culture (and subcultures). Rather, there is a multiplicity of specific audiences. This phenomenon is amplified by the use of the internet. Instead, popular music is the bearer of its own imaginary worlds and imagined audiences, which may have a certain impact on the institution of society. Popular culture, which encompasses the cultures of young people, including protest cultures, is multiform, diffuse and elusive. Understanding it requires us to 'grasp the practical intelligence of ordinary people, principally in the use they make of mass production' (Cuche 2001:71). These communities are not some kind of autarkic artistic worlds, irreconcilable musical clans. Rather, there is a circulation or circularity of influences and, from this perspective, the success of these musical styles appears to be cyclical.

Theoretically, we can admit that there is cooperation/complementarity between manufacturers and users/consumers of musical products, which themselves convey representations of society. The Ivorian music world is unique in that it is made up of a myriad of experts who participate in a cooperative network to transform the original idea into the finished product. They all have an idea of the tastes and expectations of the public, of what '*works*', of what will '*hit*' and so forth.

Musicians who have learned 'on the job' and other music school graduates can work together to produce music. In reality, they are all involved in this intuitive marketing. And this marketing (or rather this intuitive knowledge based on their experience and common sense) comes into play in the very production of fashionable songs. The studios form a kind of vast network in which the companies (individual or nodule) are both in a position of competition and complementarity, emulation and cooperation. All this forms a complex set of social and professional networks, both physical and digital, forming a networked tribe whose origins are still unknown. These mushrooming micro-companies, often parasitic, sometimes saprophytic, can spring up just about anywhere: for example, in the domestic family sphere (an outbuilding, a room in the house, etc.).

It's true that Ivorian music is formed, made and produced elsewhere in the diaspora: in Ghana, in Accra, in Nigeria, in Lagos (see Eba Aka and Ernesto Djédjé – or how typically Ivorian music is made outside Côte d'Ivoire ...) in France, in Paris, for example, in recording studios frequented by African musicians. There, musicians of different ethnic origins rub shoulders and work as a group, driven by the same objective and the same passion: African music. Real 'paradigmatic' teams were formed, with names that come up often: Aladji Touré, Sissi Dipoko, Jimmy Hyacinthe, and Slim Pezin. The diasporic experience contributed to the formation and transformation of Ivorian music and gave it its current form. It creates a break or rupture between a before and an after, between here and there (Ricci 2016:13). (Ivorian) music is the product of a cultural cross-fertilisation in which digital media and cyberspace are important insofar as they are also places where Ivorian popular music(s) are formed and performed. They are also places where Ivorian musicians express themselves, thus producing a metadiscourse that sheds light on, or rather complicates, our understanding of the musical universe and the (social and economic) logics at work within it.

6 Music Creation and Technology

Most of the peoples who make up today's Côte d'Ivoire had polysemous terms for music, generally encompassing 'a plurality of aesthetic practices including dance, song, poetry, storytelling and everything to do with entertainment and play' (Dédy 1984:109). Creation is understood here as the act of creating a new model, an original work (Petit Larousse). It is understood as an original production or work created by one or more people. We therefore expect something new, original and authentic. Art, particularly musical art, is often seen as a 'gift' and the ability to create it as proof of this gift. The artist is seen as consecrated, and talent and success are even often said to have 'a mystical origin' (Séry 2015:61). Creativity, fertility and productivity are further proof of this gift. Ernesto Djédjé used to say of his rivals: '*kômou nè blà doblé fa sou nan* [the turaco will never become a nightingale]'. Great singers compare themselves to nightingales. No matter how hard his rivals tried, they could never match him, for '*dagbasouè nèn bla glopè zo* [The tree trunk [that floats] in the water will never become a caiman (crocodile)]'.

An art world is a structure of collective activity in which often numerous actors cooperate in complex networks to produce works of art. These works of art come into being and exist thanks to this cooperation, and always bear the traces of it (Becker 1988:27–28). Following this logic, we were interested in the 'forms of cooperation implemented' to produce music. It therefore seemed imperative to identify the constraints that the organisation places on production, to take account of the characteristics of this world of music and the way in which this operation influences (the form and content of) the music produced and therefore the end products made available to the consuming public (disseminated for the benefit of the public). Imagination permeates all human activities.

But the notion of a network can lead us to lose sight of the fact that in this universe, in this milieu of inter-acquaintance, where entrepreneurship is developing, there are alliances but also rivalries. Admittedly, this fact is far from new: the *tohourous report* rivalries between themselves. They prepare themselves mystically so as not to be defeated by their opponents. The sorcery attack is also present. A singer can 'tie up the mouth' or 'block the throat' of his rival to prevent him from singing, or even stifle his inspiration and inhibit his creativity. Singers then look for occult protections, 'medicines' – their rival can harm their performance by attacking their spectacular performances, ipso facto ruining their reputation and ultimately their career. In some cases, the sorcerous attack can even be fatal, leading to the artist's death. This is what *tohourou* Lago Liadé Émile says in his tribute song, his funeral oration, to master *tohourou* Srolou Gabriel: evil sorcerers killed him: '*A hé godogouwan* [evil sorcerers] *a yè tou o!* /A *kô lba Sérié Gossi a yè nou to bheu* (You killed Séri Gossi [another name for Srolou Gabriel] we're finished)!'

A *tohourou* singer who succeeds in performing against rivals is seen as a powerful man. His self-presentation places him in the role of 'truth-teller' and also sounds like a challenge to others. This self-presentation, very typical of traditional *tohourou* singers, is echoed by the modern popular music singer Amédée Pierre, whose nicknames, mottos or currency names all evoke the great singer he embodies and sound like challenges to his rivals. This self-presentation is reminiscent of the declamation (declension) of the griot's identity (Camara 1992; Niane 1960). These songwriters 'prepare' themselves (in an occult way) before their performance, adorning themselves with fetishes so that their rivals do not cast a spell on them or 'bind' their voices. In the words of singer Ernesto Djédjé: *'Bhle bhle nè wa sronon nikpè/ kossou gui yê wro gba lé/ Manè yè pinekpa grinè a ziri gba ziri?* [You can't teach someone to sing/ It's in the family/ (so) Why go to the fetishists (implied to block my mouth)?]'. Witchcraft, this 'living reality' of our society (Gadou 2011), invites itself into musical performance and even intervenes in unprecedented or unexpected ways. Musicians, whether 'traditional' or 'modern', often seek mystical 'protection'. After all, 'this is Africa' (Leimdorfer 2006; Djédjé 2005). Magic and witchcraft, whatever one may say, remain living realities (Boa 2010; Gadou 2011). It is therefore conceivable that they are present in the Ivorian musical (art) world.

Today, music is made in a craft with the *home studio at* its epicentre, where digital sound recording technology reigns. Technique (technology) 'is an active means of producing art [which] contributes to the establishment of mediations' (see Hennion & Latour 1996:238–239). It interferes in the daily lives of young musicians. It is becoming increasingly important for learning, creating/manufacturing, reproducing, broadcasting and listening to music. The internet and these technologies are already part of their world. They don't expect much from the state. Their musical universe, especially among novices, is characterised by resourcefulness and a certain amateurism (in the positive or 'noble' sense) at the theoretical, practical and material levels (with very approximate knowledge of harmony, organology, etc.). The socio-technical framework of musical poetics is still fairly rudimentary. These novices are '*coached*' by '*arrangers*' ... Technology, in music production (literally), invites humans to 'embrace and relate to technologies as things and relationships that complement us as much as they do not' (Nyamnjoh 2019:282). ICTs are the real *Juju* (Nyamnjoh 2019) that makes musical works possible. Here, technology and 'witchcraft' both refer 'to a world of infinite possibilities – a world of presence in simultaneous multiplicities and eternal powers to redefine reality' (Nyamnjoh 2020:282).

That said, the work of art depends less on technique than on the social construct that gives it originality and legitimacy (Rouzé 2004: 45; Hennion & Latour 1996). Indeed, a musical work (like any artistic work) can be seen as 'the ambiguous product of a struggle between the subjectivity of the artist and the technical necessities of the material' (Passeron 1999:271), where technique (digital technology) comes into play. The work that emerges (from this process) is not the product of an individual creator but rather of a collective entity working in (home)studios (which flourish here and there) where working conditions are not always optimal (compared to North American or European studios). Music is one of the best places to apply advanced technologies. These play an important role in creation (production), even if they do not guarantee creativity.

Oré Tapé Félix, *Tohourou* from Digbapia in the Daloa region, explained the elements of the costume he wears for his stage performances. The cowrie shell headband around his head is designed to inspire his creativity. The clothes he wears for his artistic performances are a legacy from his late uncle, *Tohourou* Gabriel Srolou, known as 'Gabi Show', and are supposed to provide him with both magical protection and creative inspiration. But it all starts with a 'raw' idea. The sources of inspiration are numerous and by definition unlimited. Popular artists draw their inspiration from their social environment (e.g. DJ Lewis's 'Avian Flu'), from ordinary everyday life ('Premier gaou' by Magic System), from the smallest facts of ordinary daily life. They may deal with seemingly insignificant issues told in a lapidary fashion, but are thus clearly and unambiguously a testimony to everyday life (Mouchtouris 2007:139). In any case, these songs always represent commercial opportunities.

The workshop, the rehearsal room and the recording studio are liminal spaces (Turner 1969[1997]) where music is made and where creativity is stimulated by group work. This production can take the form of musical bricolage, which requires inventiveness (Nganguè 2009:11; Kolé 2023). Many musicians, often very limited in terms of both instrumental and theoretical mastery, offer 'raw material' that will be transformed by the 'arranger' during work sessions in the (home)studio. This 'liminal being' (Turner) performs several functions (sound engineer, programmer, coach, instrumentalist, etc.) and is, in the final analysis, a veritable 'one-man band'. Some are even involved in *live* music. Technical 'mastery' is a veritable cultural (rather technical) capital in the sense of Bourdieu (1992). But this liminal being, a character wearing many hats, also serves as a role model and motivator, a stimulator, and so forth. In this world, jazz musicians, often self-taught, are 'studio sharks', sought after for their ability to add creativity. In the minds of Ivorian musicians, jazzmen represent the pinnacle of musical art, even if they can sometimes seem 'esoteric'.

The apparent paucity of sources of inspiration is due to the fact that it is subject to food preoccupations. Artists, manipulated by their stomachs, produce what will feed them. Ideological aberrations restrict the depth of questioning, reduce musicians' capacity to question, and dry up the sources of inspiration: the sources of inspiration become one-track thinking or harmless ditties.

The musician loses his 'capacity for interpellation' (Mbembe 1985:144). The pressure of producers and the 'market' must also be taken into account (even at that time). What's more, they were inexorably drawn towards '*gombos*'.

Musical creation, in these 'creative (interconnaissance) milieus' translates how and why the poet-singer narrates social life and expresses this world at the same time as constructing it, and can 'unmask, behind appearances, the languages of the powers and their codes' (Goerg 1999:6). A stable, theorising *doxa* constitutes 'a background, a back-world or even a pre-text as well as a context, a permanent accompaniment to artistic manifestations [because the doxa is] directly the driving force, or at least the medium that indirectly shapes, through its expectations, the way of thinking about and producing art' (Cauquelin 1999:12). It naively receives, assembles and mixes the most diverse conceptions. The musical work is based on cultural and unnatural patterns of perception (Caune 1995:111), which are themselves an integral part of the musical situation. The commercial profitability of the work appears (always more or less) as an imperative.

The extreme example of the *tohourou* and its magical artefacts illustrates the extent to which creativity is the real obsession of creators, and the fixation on new technologies is often aimed at compensating for the lack of ideas, the drying up of creativity which often takes the path of authenticity and which seems to creators to be a guarantee of success. 'For poetics, the dual authenticity of the material processed and the subject who acts remains an essential value' (Passeron 1999:273). However, there is a certain 'antinomy of merchandise and authenticity' (Warnier 1994:12). Authentic merchandise (be it musical) is paradoxical, marked by money, and yet guarantees 'a "personalisation" made increasingly necessary by the commodification of the universe in which we live' (Warnier 1994:20).

Because of Côte d'Ivoire's recent history, the demand for authenticity takes place in a social space where ethno-cultural identities play an important role. Authenticity, an often obsessive African quest, can be sought on the fringes of identity fiction, referring to the past, to 'tradition', to the 'typical', and so on. This (re)conquest of authenticity, beyond folklore, in those years, evokes the very opposite of a modernity deemed alienating. Some Ivorian musical promotions bet on authenticity at the risk of seeing it converted into a niche (in the marketing sense of the term) in order to 'make money'. This so-called authenticity seems more like a niche market than a serious claim to identity.

In the globalised music market, the roles of music lovers, influencers and consumers are differentiated. The development of mass media and the Internet affect the aesthetics and tastes of audiences and, logically, are likely to determine production itself to some extent. This inevitably raises the question of authenticity in terms of the distinction between 'avant-garde' and 'junk', which symbolises the triumph of profit that garrotes culture (Adorno 1962:20). Cultural creativity is not confined to a nation in the limited sense of the term, but extends to the very notions of métissage and miscegenation, the dimensions of belonging. These popular musics, born of cultural blends and reinvented traditions, are made using both complex musical technologies and re-appropriated ancestral instruments, and are part of the same movement of renewal. Despite the use of electronics and digital technology, modern popular music seems to be more about continuity than rupture. 'We live by legacies, and on legacies … elements from the past weigh and condition the present and the future to some extent' (Dollfus 2007:47).

By seeking an 'Ivorian authenticity' – which we thought was emerging with *zouglou* – Ivorian music is at the same time accompanying the construction and contradictions of identity (i.e. identity of similarity and identity of difference). Like art in general, music 'integrates the new from what has gone before, making the two coexist *as if* nothing had changed. An *as if* that defines fiction, the imaginary' (Meyer 1997:43). This quest for authenticity is also expressed in the ideals of fusion subsumed in the expression 'tradi-moderne', a word formed from traditional and modern, which, when added to 'music', refers to 'that which combines traditional and modern music' (Massoumou & Queffélec 2007:419). It can be inspired by traditional music and combine modern (European) instruments (Kua-Nzambi Toko 2018). Many musicians have felt or are feeling this absolutely reflexive need to stop, if only temporarily, in order to consider what the traditional African aesthetic – that of their environment or 'terroir' – should contribute to their contemporary modern creation. This is perhaps what is reflected in the neologism 'tradi-moderne'.

But there are still questions about the authenticity of modern Ivorian popular music, which draws on a variety of local traditions as well as, and above all, Western ones (in terms of harmony, composition, orchestration, etc.). Given all the circulation of forms, ideas, materials and people, all the exchanges, all the revivals, all the mixes – can we really still talk about authenticity? Like tradition, which is invented, authenticity is produced by the mobility of people, ideas and objects. Authenticity, like tradition, is dynamic. One way of being 'original' is to draw on the reservoir of 'traditional' music, the music of the 'terroir'. This means mixing or revisiting it in the light of Western musical traditions, popular music from Northern countries, and other African music such as Congolese *rumba*, *highlife*, *makossa* and so on. This justifies the names of mixes such as '*zézé pop*', '*aloukou pop*', '*ziglibithy-makossa*' and so on. The 'cosmopolitan nativism' (Olaniyan 2004), a veritable endogenous 'cosmopolit-anism', can also be found in a musician like Meiway. This act of gentle resistance to Euro-American cultural imperialism is not closed in on itself or turned in on ancestrality, but rather open to intentional and egalitarian hybridisation, by no means as a result of coercion or capitulation to foreign cultural hegemonic forces. However, 'authenticity is illusory if rationality remains alien to it in every respect, if it is not expressed through the instrumentalities of technology which, when mastered, can provide it with the necessary, though not sufficient, conditions' (Eboussi Boulaga 1977:228). What can musical 'authenticity' really be if it is left to the laws of a music market driven by profit?

'Technology', which is revealed (imposed) fairly early on in the musician's life, is central to understanding the musical poietic process. In the Ivorian music world, musicians find it extremely difficult to obtain quality instruments and make do as best they can. The most numerous and '*affordable*' musical instruments and electronic equipment come from Asia, with China supplanting European 'domination'. Instruments made in Japan, and *even more so* in the United States, often remain out of reach, and are the stuff of fantasy for professionals and well-informed amateurs. There is still the informal second-hand market offering instruments from France. Technology is still involved in the very use of these tools to produce musical works and record them. Music is probably the art form that the new media, recording techniques, sound synthesis and data transmission are turning most upside down (Tesser 2006).

Music, which was already highly electronic and 'mechanised', has gone through a computerised phase. This change began about thirty years ago. This modernity is then expressed by its formidable capacity to appropriate the old musical heritage (sounds, rhythms, instruments, lyrics) thanks in particular to *sampling*. So, with these samples, taken from what is real but not necessarily new, we produce something else, something new but not necessarily new. 'Technology' offers a lot of 'prefabricated' material. In the Ivorian music world today, most people under thirty have little or no musical training. They 'master' technology, 'cracking' *software on* the Internet, and so on. They compose from patches, but they don't know how to use them. They compose using *patches*, *loops*, musical loops (and to a certain extent, artificial intelligence). That said, they often use African musicians as their reference point. They are on the internet, in digital social networks, sharing the same images, the same videos, and with the same culture, the same imagination as the African artists of *coupé décalé* or *afrobeats,* for example, whom they adore. They haven't experienced the music of the 1970s, 1980s and so on. They compose directly from the 'prefabricated'. Thanks to new computer equipment and processes, electronic sounds produced by synthesisers (*patches*), samples or extracts of existing music or 'natural' sounds taken out of their context, can be reused to make up other sound ensembles, form repetitive sound loops (*loops*), and so on. These elements, designed for (trained) non-musicians, are often even downloadable (free of charge) from the Internet, and allow intuitive, non-linear composition, forcing 'scholastics' to adapt to the new situation.

Their relatively close elders, an 'intermediate' generation, often in their forties and fifties, have a certain culture, firstly theoretical, and then this culture of *pop* music, *rock, funk, variety, jazz,* and so on. They know how to use new technologies to express their creativity and try to combine the two, namely this overall 'musical culture' and the resources of technology. Finally, another line, by far the most numerous, calls itself 'tradi-modern' and is made up of those who play – in fact translate – what they call 'traditional' music on modern instruments, often using Western musical codes.

In reality, the most difficult thing is to put theoretical and musical knowledge, as well as technology, at the service of creativity. Either you use the 'prefabricated', or you modify (you are able to modify) the *loops* and, thanks to all the African instrument *patches* and rhythmic loops, you are able to create African music. It's easy to see how the possibilities are endless, and how an African musical authenticity, an Africanity of music, can be reconstructed from Western sound *patches* and musical loops. The 'digital revolution', and in particular the mobile Internet, is driving a transformation of cultural industries worldwide. But the Ivorian context, still strongly marked by the informal music economy and a scarcity of labels, 'is part of a service economy outside the copyright system' (Olivier 2020:98). However, music is produced for the music market, with its fashions and trends (among both producers and consumers), as well as its different 'segments' (Ivorian diaspora, African diaspora, etc.), which are important for understanding the dynamics of 'local' music. The relative inflation of publishing houses is not in itself a new phenomenon: 'The omnipotence of the distribution mechanisms available to aesthetic junk and depraved cultural goods, as well as the socially created predispositions of listeners, have, in late-stage industrial society, brought radical music into complete isolation' (Adorno 1962:15).

For producers, a record is above all 'a consumer product like any other'. In the Ivorian (African) music market, which is still relatively unorganised, most producers are both 'publishers' and 'managers' of artists. They can work with independent distributors. Distribution remains difficult, however, because of piracy (a parallel economy that deals a blow to local cultural industries) and the difficulties of internet access and its still high cost.

Ultimately, the production of modern popular music depends on the success of the work produced. More prosaically, it has to 'work'. But what is the market for *mapouka,* with its illicit videos, for *DJs,* for *coupé décalé* and its ethos of showing off, for *zouglou,* with its disorientated youth, or for *reggae,* with its

indefatigable prophets? By indigenising culture, the modernity driven by globalisation is helping to reinforce the 'indigeneity' of African and Ivorian music
(it has to sound African and Ivorian for it to sell). Urban music has become
a global phenomenon – and popular music itself is a global phenomenon. With
the power of commercial marketing, popular music has become a commodity
that must generate profits for its producers. It generally represents a market
governed by the record industry's *major companies*, with small record companies struggling to make do.

Experience of the poietics of the products of the Ivorian musical (craft)
industry shows that music is created and developed in a bricolage (technical
and identity-based) that transcends binary analyses of traditional/modern, inter-
ior/exterior, rural/urban. In these creative adventures driven by passion and
dreams of success and glory, the pieces of music are constructed over the course
of the performances by the various contributions of the (many or diverse)
contributors, who are de facto co-authors or co-composers. As for success in
this musical universe, the Ivorian music world in the process of professionalisation resembles a social field in many respects (Bourdieu 1992:28).

7 Professionalisation or the Search for '*Gombos*'?

The world of music is becoming ever more demanding and its 'market' ever
more competitive. The professionalisation and professionalism of the players
at both methodical and technical levels are a must. This is the price to pay for
safeguarding the national cultural heritage, which is at the heart of the Ivorian
government's development strategy. Professionalism refers to imported
and often copied structures, operations and procedures. Due to a lack of
appropriate training, professionalism is still lacking among the players, and
the titles they use ('manager', 'producer', 'executive producer', 'artistic director',
'arranger', or even 'artist') are mainly part of their '*look*'. The young artist-
musician often even begins to create his appearance as an artist before he has
mastered his art.

The Ivorian music world is marked by the collaboration of high-level amateurs and professionals. A division of labour, notably between author and
lyricist, composer, 'musician (musicist)', interpreter and performer (Vian
1997:13; Agawu 2016:4) can help to grasp the phenomenological reality of
the tasks and responsibilities of the actors in the musical art world. Each
category of actor involved in the production of a musical work has 'a bundle
of tasks to accomplish. Although the division of tasks is to a large extent
arbitrary (it could have been done differently, and it is only based on the
agreement of all or most of the participants), it is not easy to modify for all

that' (Becker 1988: 37). But this division is tending to be blurred because the combination of these tasks is frequent and facilitated by the mastery of technology. The mass internet has ushered in an era of democratisation of skills, following on from political and educational democratisation. The main difference between the mass media and the web is that, on the web, amateurs take centre stage: 'the contemporary web has become the kingdom of amateurs' (Flichy 2010:7). Amateur is understood here as both producer and consumer (Flichy 2010:13). A (very) strong presence of amateurs at all levels of the music production chain. In this world, do-it-yourself is the order of the day, and the artist (the actor) appears as a master builder who finds himself at several points in the production chain of this cultural product. Singers are often simultaneously composers, arrangers and authors of the texts they perform.

The intervention of technology does not cancel out the artisanal aspect of music production, and the making of popular music appears to be a veritable production craft combining new and old technologies. For players who are often penniless and live by their wits, professionalism is first and foremost a question of survival. The quest for '*gombos*', small emoluments to 'tide them over', illustrates the overall precariousness of the musical world, made up of players who are still poorly organised and unaware of their rights. This need for 'gombo', which drives people from one genre (or style) to another, is a driving force behind the (still embryonic) professionalisation of the Ivorian music scene. Popular music has enabled some young people to move from the status of 'unemployed' or 'small-time earners' with little status, to that of 'artist', which is more rewarding. Along with football, it is a symbol of success for young people, and its singing heroes are heralds of a politically, socially and economically dominated group. 'Breakthrough' in music is a dream come true. *Breaking into* music is a dream for many young people, almost as much as becoming an international footballer, and remains the ineffable hope of many. They enter and find themselves in a world where the competition is increasingly fierce, and where it is more and more difficult to make a name for oneself, hence the temptation to consider this world as a 'social field' (Bourdieu 1984: 113–116). Evolving in the world of musical art therefore involves forging alliances. Having a certain mastery of the new technologies (the new *jujus*) is an asset for existing in and promoting productions and performances.

Although few in number, record labels (e.g. Badmos) play a key role in both the 'authenticity' and commercial exploitation of musical heritage. Authenticity is becoming increasingly fantasised. Today, given the great mobility of people, Chinese furniture is '*made in France*' by French people and Asian immigrants to make it look 'typically' Chinese (Warnier 1994:13–14; Julien 1994:30). There is a good chance that the African diviner's cowrie shells are Chinese.

Similarly, 'typically' Ivorian music is often recorded outside Côte d'Ivoire (in Ghana, Nigeria, France, the USA, etc.) by a motley crew of musicians, few of whom are actually Ivorians. So what constitutes typicality, in this case Ivorian musicality? As a commodity, it is authenticated and guaranteed by a kind of stereotypical sound, imbued with a certain typicity, which in turn refers back to the Ivorian musical imagination. After all, it comes from the industrialised West. Designed and above all manufactured abroad, in a developed country, this musical merchandise has something exotic about it as well as (good) quality. 'It is by using the market as a springboard that the exotic object, claiming an authenticity [here, Ivorian], can bounce back into the present of mass consumption' (Warnier 1994a:13). Authenticity is (something) cobbled together. In the logic of culture-tradition, the guarantee of authenticity is linked to (stems from) a ritualised and codified process of recognition by peers and acceptance by the 'people', where music as such has no (real) market value. Today, it is the reputation of record labels, in particular the fame of artists' managers, the audience of 'cultural' journalists, the popularity of radio and television presenters, the 'aggressiveness' of show promoters, the authority of music analysts (academics of all stripes and backgrounds), in short all these actions which, in some way aggregated, contribute to the 'certification' of the authenticity of modern popular music by making it worthy of interest. To this must be added recognition by peers (or by an influential peer) within (or in the networks of) what have been described earlier (somewhat abusively) as musical 'tribes'. So, for example, the legitimising and authenticating authority for *reggae* is Jamaica par excellence, that imaginary diasporic Ethiopia, and in particular Kingston, which is an object of adoration for *reggae-men*. Alpha Blondy's trip to Kingston, as the video clip shows, serves as much as a pilgrimage to the 'source' as it does a test of authentication, validation, completion and elevation of his *reggae* by what represents the supreme place of creation of this musical genre.

In all lucidity, we have to admit that 'musical domination' is exercised with the complicity, or rather perhaps the cooperation, of the 'dominated' (Hennion 1981). Many musicians, inspired by what is happening especially in the United States in Afro-American and increasingly Nigerian circles, are tempted to create labels, often ephemeral, living only for the duration of a '*single*', veritable self-promotion labels whose outdated traces can be found on this or that album or from time to time on the Internet.

Until recently, Côte d'Ivoire, like many African countries, did not make intellectual property (scientific, literary and artistic) a priority. Colonial legislation in this area lasted well beyond the colonial period itself. The body responsible for such rights, the Bureau ivoirien des droits d'auteurs (BURIDA), broadly modelled on the French Société des auteurs compositeurs et éditeurs de musique (SACEM), began operations in April 1981. There were at least two reasons for this slowness: (i) the State gave priority to the economy and (ii) 'the players in the cultural sector, faced with many other difficulties, paid little attention to the notion of copyright' (Pierrat 2005). Even today, legislation remains silent on many points (e.g. publishing contracts and the legal regime applicable to cross-border co-publications).

The Bureau ivoirien des droits d'auteurs, which still operates as an ad hoc society of authors, currently manages the rights of more than 6,000 authors, producers and internet artists, and more than 72,000 works. The artist declares his work to BURIDA, which manages the copyright. In return, it benefits from the distribution of the funds collected. These rights (or '*royalties*') constitute the remuneration of the author, producer or songwriter. For political, economic and socio-cultural reasons, the Office is faced with real difficulties in administering (recording, monitoring, redistributing, archiving, managing, etc.) the rights of songwriters and composers in Côte d'Ivoire (Kossonou 2020).

Because of their overwhelming numbers, the musicians de facto dominate BURIDA. Bureau ivoirien des droits d'auteurs is not really equipped to control broadcasting. Instead, this task is performed by the High Authority for Audiovisual Communication. It is easy to understand the scale of the difficulties that arise: 'music broadcasting gives rise to a dispute between orchestras and singers on the one hand, and on the other, many radio stations that do not pay the former their royalties; the radio stations, however, ensure or maintain the success of many artists' (Tudesq 2002:187).

Under such conditions, it seems difficult to protect the wealth of folklore (traditional works and artists, intellectual property of Indigenous peoples) and more broadly cultural heritage through intellectual property. Some even believe that Ivorians themselves should exploit this cultural wealth so that it does not come back to us in the form of prefabricated manufactured products to be used in the creation of 'typically' Ivorian music, while keeping us in a situation of dependence on Western producers of musical goods and products.

It is clear that, in many cases, the traditional social institutions safeguarding the rights of traditional cultural producers have been shattered by the upheaval of the social order brought about by colonisation. The post-colonial state – particularly the body responsible for copyright – is struggling to integrate them into its modus operandi. It is clear (though difficult to accept) that the intangible assets of ancient traditional cultural agents (commonly known as folklore), regarded as anonymous and collective, are at worst illegitimately appropriated, at best cannibalised (see Diawara 2015; Röschenthaler 2015).

The context for the development and creation of the performing arts is changing, with the creation of labels, (*home*)recording studios, networks of professionals and concert venues. The sector is becoming more professional, with a kind of mass production by craftsmen. For any musician (whether a beginner or not), a fundamental problem is that of local and, if possible, international visibility. This is achieved through recordings (Olivier 2020) and the various opportunities to be seen and heard, particularly through the media. The Market for African Performing Arts (MASA) was created to promote and develop African performing arts both locally and globally. It creates a festive space for stage performances and meetings (between artists, presenters and promoters), and subsequently a lever for raising the profile of artists and their work. However, it has not been as successful as expected in terms of attendance, audience engagement and loyalty, and promotional and commercial spin-offs. This is probably due to a strategy that is still ill-suited to the lability of the market for artistic and cultural products (Doua 2009).

Artists have a complex relationship with the state media (Land 1995) and the commercial media. The latter have played an undeniable role in the 'modernisation' of men, the popularisation of Ivorian culture and its opening up to the outside world (Land 1992). *Volens nolens,* the mass media (state or commercial) remain the royal road to success for these musicians, but it remains largely inaccessible. A musician appearing on television is likely to end up on the web (the reverse is not always true). The traditional mass media remain star-making machines. They can offer platforms to musicians who get noticed and stand out on web platforms.

Today, 'membership of social networks also enables [young artists] to develop their talent. They become part of different social circles that provide them with the resources they need to realise their dream: to promote their musical talent and gain notoriety' (Asinome 2017:177). With Internet platforms, a digital transformation is underway in Côte d'Ivoire. Artistic creation – particularly musical creation – is affected by commercial networking via the Internet. This is the path currently being taken by 'young talent' in need of funding. They see free web platforms (*YouTube, SoundCloud*, even *Facebook*, etc.) as public virtual spaces for promoting their art and building an artistic identity to try to enter a cultural market that has become highly competitive and launch their careers. They hope, through '*views*', '*likes*', '*shares*' and even positive comments, if not to create a *buzz*, at least to interest a producer or benefactor. Social networks are therefore of real importance in winning over an audience, a public, a 'market'.

The traditional mass media are adapting as much as possible to the new context created by new technologies by setting up websites and social networking platforms offering all or part of their programmes for free listening. The great diversity of these programmes has often been mistaken for clear evidence of the cultural imperialism of which Côte d'Ivoire (like many other countries) was a victim. The programmes could even be condemned as vectors of cultural alienation.

Technology is bringing about spatio-temporal changes, particularly in the speed of access, production and distribution it offers. The very way in which music is created has changed, bringing with it a new relationship between creators and consumers, both to the world of music and to music itself. The desire to succeed has led to expatriation, particularly to Europe, to places where '*art is considered*', where talent can be developed and where artistic expression can flourish.

The social status and social condition of the artist, past and present, are critical sites of cultural heritage. In traditional society, the artist, the chanson-nier, enjoyed (and still enjoys) an honourable status – an honourability that is above all symbolic (Séry 2015; Tapé 1986:149–151). In Nubian Africa, art was not considered the preserve of a secret society. From this came 'a profound affirmation of people's belief in the indivisibility of art and society' (Achebe 1973:620). The expression 'Nubian Africa' (coined by Cheik Anta Diop), whose supposed unity is borrowed from theories of Africanness, has the advantage of de-racialising and de-physicalising an Africa still characterised by its ancient and modern observers as a race and an ecosystem. It also makes it possible to characterise Africa 'in terms of social and cultural history, in short, in anthropological terms' (Memel-Fotê 1991:1).

In traditional African society, music, 'conceived as a high ideological instance', functioned as a socio-cultural support tool at key moments in ritual life (initiation, marriage, funerals) and in the economic and political spheres: 'the omnipresent and omnipotent character of this music was ensured by a certain authoritative, quasi-sacred word which, in our opinion, constitutes a further demonstration of the importance attached to art in traditional society' (Dédy 1984:113).

Moreover, the fact that 'there are no rigid barriers between the creators of culture and the consumers [and that] art belongs to everyone and is a "function" of society' (Achebe 1973:621) comes from this Nubian Africa of the holistic concern of the societies that make it up (Achebe 1973; Dédy 1986; Wondji 1986a; Séry 2015). Musical performances are a good illustration of this: the Western divide between stage and audience is erased when spectators, no longer able to hold back, burst in during the concert to encourage the artist (by wiping his forehead, dancing a little with him, kissing him, giving him banknotes, etc.). Like the *bagnon of* the *Krou* societies of western and central western Côte d'Ivoire, the artist, whether a star or just passing through, is admired physically, morally and intellectually (Wondji 1986b:59, 71). The town will only show the obvious side, that of the entertainer, the one without whom, despite everything, the party cannot be complete.

Today's artist-musicians face serious problems of recognition both during their lifetime and posthumously. Many of their works are illegally exploited. This is much more widespread than one might imagine, and does not only concern so-called 'traditional' or 'local' musicians, who are often poorly trained, but also eminent musicians with established international reputations, as in the case of Manu Dibango (cf. Pajon 2021:54–55).

While the artist may enjoy a degree of honour, even symbolic, his or her social status is often precarious. Today, the singer-musician is often regarded as a 'poor soul', at best a penny-pincher, bohemian, unserious, flighty. His portrait as a balladeer is not very glowing. The artist-musician remained vulnerable, and many of them fell into decay and oblivion without ever having achieved fame or fortune. Appeals for charity for the health problems of this or that musician are frequently in the press. The outcome is usually fatal, and the artist dies destitute (Séry 2015). In short, while the musician-artist, past and present, enjoys a certain prestige, his or her 'social condition' is still generally one of precariousness. This condition resurfaces at the death or funeral of a particular artist. But the problem transcends time and remains virtually unchanged.

Generally speaking, there is a continuity between the popular music of yesterday and that of today. This continuity tends to be disrupted by the use of technology.

8 Between Entertainment and Popular Intellectuality

An in-depth examination of the points of rupture and continuity between the 'traditional' singer and the 'modern' singer shows that popular intellectuality constitutes the true cultural heritage of music. The music changes, but the heritage remains, ensuring a kind of artistic/intellectual continuity in the art of music. The modern popular song, elusive and untameable, is a place where popular intellectuality is expressed by singer-artists considered to be popular intellectuals.

Popular music was also the 'overlord' of entertainment. Ordinary festive places marked by fusion, effusion and confusion, the excesses of orgiasm, become popular means of disseminating popular music and bringing it into contact with the population. These non-places (Augé 1992), veritable places of enchantment (Winkin 2001), liminoid spaces (Turner 1988), are also places where artists-singers perform. Performed music, a living spectacle, restores and mobilises the physicality of the spoken word, unlike writing. Modern popular song thus reflects the heritage of the 'traditional' storyteller/musician and the question of the 'message' or 'moral' of the story being told, and how this fits in with the (bizarre) democratic order.

The artist is, physically or through the mediation of the recording, at once the master, the host, the soul, the spirit, the breath of the party (Duvignaud 1991). He is a liminal being (Turner 1969[1997]) in the same way as (*home*)studio arrangers. He gives of himself and his talent. The affirmation of the gift lies in the idea that 'the link is more important than the material [good]' (Caillé 2007:9). Giving implies alliance and communion. The artist (in this case the musician) 'gives' to others something that may be the gift of self or the gift of speech. Artistic speech is an immemorial means by which 'man has always used art as a means of becoming aware of the highest ideas and interests of his mind. Peoples have deposited their highest conceptions in the productions of art, have expressed them and have become aware of them by means of art' (Hegel ed. 1964:12–13). The artist-singer, guardian of moral values (Tapé 1986b), offers the world the object of his creative inspiration, the fruit of his reflections, his thoughts. Yet they remain attached to what they 'give', because there is always something of themselves in their work. This gift of knowledge and/or self contains a link. The artist-musician is this human benefactor who, by giving his life and labour to the community, manifests 'the joy of giving in public, the pleasure of generous artistic expenditure; the pleasure of hospitality and of private and public celebration', following an enduring principle: 'to come out of oneself, to give, freely and obligatorily' (Mauss 1925[2012]:216–222). What's more: 'If we give things and return them, it's because we give and return *each other* "respects" – we still say "courtesies". But it's also because we give *ourselves* by giving, and if we give *ourselves*, it's because we "owe" *ourselves* – ourselves and our property – to others' (Mauss 1925[2012]:171). It is in this way, in a logic of counter-giving itself calling for emulation-competition/ competition between (counter-)givers, that we can explain/understand the (re)actions, burlesque in appearance, of the audience (see above) who come into direct contact with the performer.

The artist-musician is the 'man of the people', a kind of folk hero whose philosophy is based primarily on faith in the social group to which he belongs, because 'in a diffuse way, he thinks things the way he does: the man of the people thinks that such a large mass cannot be so completely wrong' (Gramsci 1983:154). This is what makes the artist a voice of the people.

Like the folk tale, the song of the *tohourou* or the melody of the chansonnier, the modern folk song tells an entertaining story, can 'create a spectacle that is at the same time a place of truth. Of course, the story (*fabula*) changes, since it depends on circumstances and other more or less controlled events' (Bahi 1994:251). The modern singer pulls 'strings' from all possible repertoires, borrowing procedures, formulas, allegories and metaphorical subtleties from the traditional masters of the spoken word for his sung narratives.

Popular music *in the broadest sense of the term* is also the expression of a popular intellectuality. The expression 'popular intellectual' may seem surprising because it combines two apparently antinomic terms. 'Intellectuality' here refers to the fact that a person is intellectual, or to his or her ability to be intellectual. Most conceptions of the intellectual are not free of elitist considerations. The intellectual is not necessarily a Western scholar. The scholar is not necessarily an intellectual (Sartre 1972; Wondji 1986a; Séry 2015). Reflection on the intellectual is always threatened by a certain intellectualism that is itself imbued with a certain elitism.

The term 'popular' presupposes and posits the most effective language and mode of resistance (Hall 2007). A world-famous – and therefore popular – intellectual is no less an intellectual. As a result of globalisation and the ability of individuals to make themselves 'heard', no one has a monopoly on legitimate intellectual thought. The artist-musician, as a free-spirited man of the people, has a certain authority, and is often even authoritative, because people recognise his behaviour, his 'knowledge and skills', and see in him an exceptional being.

The artist-musician is the ideological and moral sentinel of society (and not just of the village from which he comes). As an intellectual born of the people, he speaks with authority by virtue of his social position. Words of authority operate 'thanks to the assistance of social mechanisms capable of producing that complicity, based on ignorance, which is at the root of all authority' (Bourdieu 1992:113). Authority refers to the social unconscious. It is 'the attestation of the order of values, representations and systems of unconscious representations to which individuals and groups refer in life' (Moreau de Bellaing 1990:62). The artist-musician is thus a non-authoritarian authority, even a 'charismatic' authority (Weber 1971[1995]:320, 325) as much as a traditional or rational authority, because of his exceptional qualities. There is a continuity between this authority operating mainly in primary sociality (on the scale of the village, neighbourhood or maquis), and that acting in secondary sociality (in global social relations) (Moreau de Bellaing 1990:58–59). The artist-musician embodies the reminiscences of an anthropological form of authority, separate from power, invested with a 'mythical' authority that legitimises his acts and (sung) words.

Thus, the (original) griot, the Bété *tohourou*, the Baoulé chansonnier and the sénoufo *djéguélés* perform educational, social, ethical and political functions (Wondji 1986b; Camara 1992; Koné 2020). However, 'no musical form carries with it the slightest political or social orientation' (Martin 2000:170), so it is a social desire to invert or convert music to this task that is at work. The griot, master of the spoken word and a plural character, strengthens the social bond 'through multiform mediation between all the actors in the community. This generally makes him a public figure and an intellectual among the intellectuals of the city' (Ouattara 2018:44). Alongside storytellers and healers, these singer-artists are part of local intellectual traditions.

Nolens volens, these artist-musicians are 'elites of intellectuals of a new type [emerging] directly from the mass out while remaining in contact with it' (Gramsci 1983:155). As an intellectual, the artist is a model for others: 'the artist of yesterday resembles the intellectual of today. He influences society through the beauty of his ideas' (Tapé 1986b:151). From the Masque chanteur, to the *Tohourou*, to the 'traditional chansonnier', then to the modern singer, there seems to be continuity rather than rupture. The popular intellectual himself is a spokesman for the people. A hero as much as a herald, heroic because heraldic, the popular singer is allowed to give advice, to teach in the public square. With a 'didactic' aim, these narrations are a mirror of society's ethical conceptions (Bahi 1994). Giving advice, teaching and moralising are often done through a diversion, in allegorical form. There are many examples. 'Several songs evoke in humorous terms the pain of Africans faced with a life they have no control over and which eludes them' (Mbembe 1985:143). Artists are not necessarily commissioned or paid to do this. They take their responsibilities.

As a performance and an artistic space, an emotive and poetic instance (Herndon 1992:164), popular song is a purveyor of 'myths' (Lévi-Strauss 1958[1974]) and is endowed with an interpellative, referential and conative capacity, hence its communicative competence. Once disseminated by the media, it lends itself easily to consciousness-raising initiatives. Popular song, an activity of the mind by artists who are often committed to delivering the fruits of their reflections in the public arena, is one of the places where popular intellec-tuality is expressed. This intellectuality is deeply rooted in culture, particularly 'tradition' (the singer-songwriter mask, etc.), whose mutations place today's mod-ern artist in a logic of continuity. With technology, the modern artist-singer remodels features of the traditional artist-singer and extends the *tekhnè* (Laye 1978; Wondji 1986b; Camara 1992): 'yesterday's artist resembles today's intellec-tual. He influences society through the beauty of his ideas' (Tapé 1986b:151).

Musician-artists can be considered as 'popular intellectuals', in the same way as street discussion leaders who call themselves 'street intellectuals' (Bahi 2013). The intellectual of the traditional milieu, the 'village intellectual' (Séry 2015:44, 46), the 'vernacular intellectual' (Farred 2003), is not the literate person of the village, the one who attended school. 'An "illiterate intellectual", he is one of the "traditionalists", "wise men" and thinkers who, along with politicians and journalists, "function as" intellectuals' (Copans 1993:8). Unlike the modern African intellectual, the illiterate 'traditional' intellectual is neither an 'outsider' among his own people (Toulabor 1993), nor the regal heir of the colonial state. Rather, he is one of its collateral victims, reduced to a 'folkloric' figure in the most depreciatory sense of the term. It has remained present in society and active at key moments in social life (celebrations, commemorations, funerals, etc.). But this reduction has, if not reduced him to symbolic death, at least neutralised his action.

Figures of popular culture, these authentic 'intellectuals from below' (Touraine 1992), can be called 'invisible intellectuals' because they are 'actors in the processes of intelligibility of the world who are not yet socially stamped and classified in a special category' (Copans 1993:17). Singers and other intermediate categories (investigative journalists), these *'practitioners of the unveiling of the reality effect are invisible intellectuals* ... sensitive to the expectations of their real, imaginary or simply potential audiences' (Copans 1993:23–24). Ultimately, whatever their training and trajectory, the characteristic of these intellectuals or thinkers is 'vernacularity', indicating 'the discursive hijacking of the accepted dominant intellectual modality and vocabulary and the adoption of a new positioning and idiomatic language' (Farred 2003:11).

Contrary to prevailing conceptions, intellectuality is not the exclusive preserve of people who are necessarily educated in Western schools, inevitably candidates for assimilation and inevitably doomed to cultural alienation. A distinction can be made between 'intellectuals' and 'technicians of practical knowledge' (Sartre 1972:16–18). These two social categories are often confused. In most conceptualisations of intellectuals, the latter takes precedence over the former. However erudite they may be, specialists in practical knowledge are not necessarily 'intellectuals'.

Today, the term 'intellectual' is somewhat overused. While they were often the soul of liberating nationalisms, they have become the blemish of the postcolonial era, going 'from the status of a badge of pride to a term of abuse and derision' (Mkandawire 2005:3). The image of the 'classical' intellectual elites from Western schools is a mixed one. They enjoy a certain prestige because of their cultural, economic, social and even symbolic capital (Bourdieu), which makes them invaluable supporters. But at the same time, they are seen as corrupt (*'they eat'*, and often *'alone'*), far removed from the concerns of ordinary people, and are therefore in a certain disgrace in people's minds. In many rural areas, they are referred to as 'Whites', illustrating the distance that separates them from their compatriots. Worse still, they are seen as accomplices, if not culprits, in the country's relative failure.

Popular intellectuals are not simply relays of 'patented' ('classic') intellectuals. They do more than simply take over from the patent intellectuals 'in the field of social criticism, while at the same time taking on the educational function traditionally assigned to them' (Albert & Kouvouama 2007:17). The novelty comes from the late discovery of this ancient cultural trait by these Western scholars and their late interest in the figure of the singer-artist. This traditional intellectual function is often overlooked in popular music research. Instead, folk singers develop an intellectuality fuelled by the currents of thought, causes and debates of their time. They fulfil a mission of popular consciousness. The exercise of this popular intellectuality, which constitutes another voice of social criticism, does not delegitimise the function and role of the 'classical' ('patented') intellectual. But this position of the popular intellectual is relatively uncomfortable because, *nolens volens,* the intellectual and the popular are in a relationship of complementarity as much as contradiction, 'a paradoxical relationship' (Albert & Kouvouama 2007).

However, the popular intellectual (coming from the people and speaking in their name), given his cultural capital and the distance thus induced, remains in a situation of exteriority and his discourse remote from the people (Albert & Kouvouama 2007:17). Singer-artists (griots, storytellers or genealogists, traditional songwriters, etc.), as scholars, custodians of traditions and creators of culture, belong to the corporation or community of intellectuals. The concept of the popular intellectual is thus part of an Indigenous definition of intellectuals 'from below' – 'traditional' society and the 'people' being dominated by (post) modern Western society. It is reinforced by a sense of cultural continuity and a reinvention of the social role of the artist.

As members of an 'interpretative community', popular intellectuals propose 'representations' of their society (Becker 2009:19). In so doing, they set themselves up as spokespersons for this community, while at the same time taking a stand. He then produces 'A report on social reality [that] is [therefore] an artefact consisting of statements of fact, based on evidence acceptable to a given audience, and interpretations of these facts, also acceptable to that audience' (Becker 2009:28). In the current conditions of production and circulation of musical works, these artists are more likely to be relays of popular social criticism (Albert & Kouvouama 2007:18). Popular music is thus one of the expressions of the infra-politics of the dominated (Scott 2009). These reports on society (these representations of society) 'are demonstrations designed to persuade their audience of something, if only by taking that something for granted' (Becker 2009:41). The way power is expressed through humour and derision conceals a great deal of violence. It echoes the expression of ordinary violence (ordinary verbal violence, street violence, etc.).

There is certainly a risk that the entertainment aspect will be perceived but not the 'didactic' one. Moreover, the step from awareness to manipulation (influence, effect-efficiency, consequence) is a short one. Modern popular music is not a manipulative device performed by musicians under orders. Through it, young popular intellectuals have discovered their mission and are fulfilling it (Fanon 1961[2002]:197) in order to influence decisions and assume their responsibilities before history (Dagri 2019b).

The artist's 'vocation is to educate men, and he must be continually vigilant in his role as guide' (Masselis 2016; Plato 1966:126–127). The singer may be a poet or a chronicler. As a poet, he deals with the general; as a chronicler, he deals with the particular. The difference between the poet and the chronicler is not one of expression, in verse or prose. Rather, 'one tells what has happened, the other what might happen; for this reason poetry is more philosophical than chronicle: poetry deals more with the general, chronicle with the particular' (Aristotle 1980).

Because of their very nature and social formation, intellectuals develop much more slowly than other social groups. 'They represent the entire cultural tradition of a people, and want to summarise and synthesise its entire history' (Gramsci 1983:100). Their mission is to be educators, teachers (Gramsci 1983:50). There is always more or less a gap between the intellectual (higher) categories and the masses (lower) categories, which makes the intellectuals' task difficult. But what is most notable is that Ivorian intellectuals (as it happens) symbolically leave a void characterised by this situation (Eboussi-Boulaga 1977). This loss of reference points and values is replaced by a technicist and economic discourse of development. This headlong rush impoverishes the debate and leaves Africans with a deep sense of backwardness and exclusive guilt. These popular intellectuals have been trying to fill this gap ever since. These popular intellectuals would somehow fulfil the authentic (true) mission of intellectuals. But would these popular intellectuals really be able to bridge the gap (the distance) between the intellectuals and the 'popular masses'? Can they escape the attempts to tame power? Power is always trying to tame the arts, and music is communication. Communication 'converts relations of brute force, always uncertain and liable to be suspended, into lasting relations of symbolic power by which we are held and to which we feel held' (Bourdieu 1997:237).

There is always something disloyal or treacherous about African criticism of Africa and Africans. Certain criticisms and self-criticisms by patent African intellectuals, endorsed and authorised by the normal science of the former coloniser, anointed by the dominators of this world, talking from the West, and quick to give lessons to Africans, play right into the hands of Western domination. The African intellectual, aware of his double game, his murky game, his concupiscence, knows that he is part of the problems he wants to solve. Popular music can play the role of 'tutor', 'adviser' or even 'censor' (Gondola 1997:58).

On the strength of their intellectuality and their charismatic authority recognised by their audience, singers can tackle all sorts of subjects, but in their own way. Musicians talk about [certain aspects of] society, talk about [certain aspects of] everyday life: song lyrics are ways of talking about society: they often contain 'relevant observations about the organisation and functioning of society [which are also] ways in which people tell others what they know about their society, or about another that interests them' (Becker 2009:18–19) and which therefore constitute what Becker describes as 'reports on society' or 'representations of society' (Becker 2009:19). This inevitably raises the question of voice and, in particular, of 'who speaks' in these 'reports' or 'representations': in our view, it is the 'popular intellectuals (or even intellectuals of the popular)'.

Songs often have allusive verses. These allusions are broad enough to include all sorts of changes and all sorts of interpretations. In this way, the artist exercises his critical reason. In fact, it is also an exercise in citizenship, or at least an exercise in citizenship. Depending on his commitment, he may engage in social criticism. Social criticism is the denunciation of the social order, authority (or power), inequalities (social, economic, etc.) or shortcomings (morals, for example). 'Social criticism criticises the established order in the name of an ideal, more "just", more "rational" order; it is a devaluation that presupposes a valorisation. It works in the same way as satire in the theatre or the novel: *castigat* (not always) *ridendo mores in* relation to an implicit norm' (Grignon 2000:106). This social criticism can take a satirical turn. Social satire is the criticism of society through mockery and caricature. Popular song lends itself well to mockery and parody.

The song can be harsh and the singer, in revolt, can rant about the harshness of life, the 'daily miseries', the 'lost hopes', and criticise the listeners themselves. She also takes the liberty, albeit cautiously, of denouncing 'the modes of accumulation of goods at work in contemporary African societies [and] the arrogance of the rich, the lessons of the lives of the poor' (Mbembe 1985:143). It is thus one of the 'social revelators' (Balandier 1985). It can be seen as the writing of a collective self, an act of revolt, in an intellectual and even scientific context marked by a certain trivialisation of the word 'globalisation'. Popular music does not legitimise the hegemonic discourse of the master, of the 'big boys', an echo of the authorised word of power. Rather, it constitutes a counter-discourse representing the voices coming from below, from the 'little people', a return of the *vox populi*.

Popular song is an expression of the anxieties and aspirations of a society, the anxieties and aspirations of the social groups that promote it. As well as being cathartic, popular song is also a means of expressing the social imagination of groups. Thus, in the examples cited earlier, singer-artists can appear as popular intellectuals, 'relays of social criticism' (Albert & Kouvouama 2007:18) and even spokespersons for protest.

Can these popular intellectuals do anything different from the 'official' intellectuals, who are often organic (Gramsci), trained in the perspective of the former colonial masters, full of diplomas and Western-centric theories, and the architects of Africa's disenchantment? 'The efforts of the colonised to rehabilitate themselves and escape the colonial bite are logically part of the same perspective as that of colonialism'. (Fanon 1961[2002]:159). Following on from this idea, the 'postcolonial' African intellectual could only really free himself from the persistent 'bite' of resilient colonialism by rallying the peasant masses. To Fanon's already broad conception of the intellectual, including what Sartre calls the 'technicians of practical knowledge' (Sartre 1972:13), we add artist-musicians, including singers. This is a kind of 'field intellectual', capable of bridging the inevitable gap between the intellectuals and the masses. That's what many singers say – 'we're in the field', which implies 'we know what's going on'. These African intellectuals, 'by the kilo', parrots, 'potted plants' raised in greenhouses, incapable of producing original thought, willingly maintaining their subaltern status (Nyamnjoh 2012) – can they speak?

They are condemned to remain in the shadow of the master (Armah 1972[1981]), at best to the mystification of the simulacrum to increase his prestige and authority over others, at worst to a perfidious ruse borrowing the resources of the Western dominator in a mystifying violence (Derrida 1966). The logic of imitation is close to that of counterfeiting. This kind of simulacrum is at the heart of the processes and procedures for seizing (or retaining) power by intellectuals drained by the bite of resilient colonialism.

Every government has its artists and 'acrobats', as well as its appointed or authorised intellectuals, when these do not simply become political players (N'Da 1999:211–212). This endorsement of Ivorian musical artists, which has varied over time, aims to exalt Ivorian pride. Power domesticates the arts. Song – the sung word – like tales, proverbs and metaphors, is a disguised form of communication. The choice of form of communication, particularly the satire that popular song readily indulges in, is crucial to correcting morals, regardless of social category or privilege, by entertaining and even mocking. The popular intellectual, 'creator [from] the people' (Mouchtouris 2007:139), often very close to their social and political expectations, is the object of covetousness. It is liable to be used or manipulated by entrepreneurs or political parties, or by those in power whose attitude to popular music (e.g. *mapouka,* sometimes consumed, sometimes censored) is ambiguous or even hypocritical. What remains is self-censorship or the love song as an outlet for freedom.

References

Achebe, C., 1973, 'Africa and her writers', *The Massachusetts Review*, Vol. 14, No. 3, (Summer), pp. 617–629.

Adorno, T. W., 1962, *Philosophie de la nouvelle musique*, Paris, Gallimard, coll. Tel.

Agawu, K., 2016, *The African Imagination in Music*, London, Oxford University Press. DOI: https://doi.org/10.1093/acprof:oso/9780190263201.001.0001.

Akindès, S., 2002, 'Playing it "loud and straight"'. Reggae, Zouglou Mapouka and youth insubordination in Côte d'Ivoire", in *Playing with Identities in Contemporary Music in Africa*, M. Palmberg and A. Kirkegaard (Eds.), Uppsala, Nordiska Afrikainstitutet, pp. 99–100.

Albert, C. & Kouvouama, A., 2007, 'Introduction. Intellectuels populaires: Un paradoxe créatif", in *Intellectuels populaires: Un paradoxe créatif*, Hervé Maupeu, Christiane Albert & Abel Kouvouama, (Eds.), Pau, PU Pau et Pays de l'Adour, pp. 17–26.

Anderson, B., 1983, *L'imaginaire national*, Paris, La Découverte.

Appadurai, A., 2001, *Après le colonialisme: Les conséquences culturelles de la globalisation*, Paris, Payot.

Arendt, H., 1972[2005], *La crise de la culture*, Paris, Gallimard, Coll. Folio essais.

Aristotle, 1980, *The Poetics*, texte, traduction, notes par Roselyne Dupont-Roc et Jean Lallot, Paris, Seuil.

Armah, A. K., 1972[1981], *Why Are We So Blest?*, London, Heinemann, African Writers Series.

Asinome, E., 2017, 'Vivre sa passion et gagner sa vie: Jeunes artistes du sud-ouest de Madagascar à la recherche de notoriété dans la capitale malgache', *Afrique et Développement*, Vol. 42, No. 2, pp. 173–191.

Augé, M., 1992, *Non-lieux. Introduction à une anthropologie de la surmodernité*, Paris, Seuil.

Babi, R., 2010, *Amédée Pierre, le dopé national, grand maître de la parole*, Paris, L'Harmattan.

Bachimon, P., 2001, 'La "rurbanité" au Centre de la Recherche: Action', *Sempervira*, No. 10, Abidjan, Centre Suisse de Recherches Scientifiques, pp. 9–12.

Bahi, A., 2021, *Il n'y a pas de crocodiles à Cocody: Anthropologie de la communication musicale en Côte d'Ivoire*, Bamenda, Langaa.

Bahi, A., 2013, *L'ivoirité mouvementée: Jeunes, médias et politique en Côte d'Ivoire*, Bamenda, Langaa.

Bahi, A., 2011, 'Musique populaire moderne et coproduction de l'imaginaire national en Côte d'Ivoire', in *Côte d'Ivoire: La réinvention de soi dans la violence*, Francis Akindès (Ed.), Dakar, Council for the Development of Social Science Research in Africa, pp. 133–168.

Bahi, A., 2010, 'Jeunes et imaginaire de la modernité à Abidjan', *Cadernos de estudos africanos*, No. 18/19, June 2009–July 2010, pp. 47–61.

Bahi, A., 1999, 'La "télé-maquis": Les images de l'homme ordinaire', *En Quête*, No. 4, pp. 9–30.

Bahi, A., 1998, 'Les "tambours bâillonnés": Contrôle et mainmise du pouvoir sur les médias en Côte d'Ivoire', *Media Development*, Vol. 45, No. 4, pp. 36–45.

Bahi, A., 1994, *Narration, traditions et modernité dans le discours filmique de Comment ça va? une émission de la Télévision Ivoirienne*, Lille, Atelier National de Réproduction des Thèses Diffusion.

Balandier, G., 2008, 'De tous temps, de tous lieux, l'information et la communication', *L'Homme*, Nos. 185–186, pp. 55–63.

Balandier, G., 1985, *Sociologie des Brazzavilles noires*, Paris, Presses de la Fnsp.

Balandier, G., 1974[1985], *Anthropo-logiques*, Paris, Le Livre de Poche.

Balandier, G., 1957, *Afrique ambiguë*, Paris, Plon, coll. Terre humaine.

Barber, K., 2018, *A History of African Popular Culture*, Cambridge, Cambridge University Press.

Barber, K., 2015, 'Authorship, copyright and quotation in oral and print spheres in early colonial Yorubaland', in *Copyright Africa: How Intellectual Property, Media and Markets Transform Immaterial Cultural Goods*, Ute Röschenthaler & Mamadou Diawarra (Eds.), Canon Pyon, Sean Kingston Publishing, pp. 101–123.

Barthes, R., 1957, *Mythologies*, Paris, Seuil.

Bassand, M., 2001, 'Les six paramètres de la métropolisation', *Cahiers de la métropolisation*, No. 1, Fiche débat, pp. 33–39.

Bauman, R., 1992, 'Performance', in *Folklore, Cultural Performances, and Popular Entertainments: A Communications-Centered Handbook*, Richard Bauman (Ed.), Oxford, Oxford University Press, pp. 41–49.

Bazin, L., 2014, 'Préface', in *Les mutuelles de développement en Côte d'Ivoire: Idéologie de l'origine et modernisation villageoise*, by Roch Yao Gbabeli, Paris, L'Harmattan, pp. ii–viii.

Becker, H. S., 2009, *Comment parler de la société: Artistes, écrivains, chercheurs et représentations sociales*, Paris, La Découverte.

Becker, H., 1988[2006], *Les mondes de l'art*, Paris, Flammarion.

Béhague, G. H., 1992, 'Musical Performance', in *Folklore, Cultural Performances, and Popular Entertainments: A Communications-Centered Handbook*, Richard Bauman (Ed.), Oxford, Oxford University Press, pp. 172–178.

Bemba, S., 1984, *Cinquante ans de musique du Congo-Zaïre, 1920–1970: De Paul Kamba à Tabu-Ley*, Paris, Présence africaine.

Bergson, H., 1936, 'Quel est l'objet de l'art?', Paris, BnF, Archives de la Parole, Service de la coopération numérique, Gallica.

Bibeau, G., 1993, 'Review of [Didier Fassin: *Pouvoir et maladie en Afrique. Anthropologie sociale dans la banlieue de Dakar*, Paris, Presses Universitaires de France, coll. Les champs de la santé, 1992, 359 pp., bibliogr.]'. *Anthropologie et Sociétés*, Vol. 17, Nos. 1–2, pp. 253–260. DOI: https://doi.org/10.7202/015260ar, 21.01.2020.

Boa, T. R., 2010, *La sorcellerie n'existe pas*, Abidjan, Les éditions du CERAP.

Boka, A., 2013, *Coupé décalé: Sens d'un genre musical en Afrique*, Paris, L'Harmattan.

Bonniol, J.-L., 1999, 'A propos de la *World Music*: Logiques de production et de réception', in *Universalisation et différenciation des modèles culturels*, Sélim Abou & Katia Haddad (Eds.), Beyrouth – Montréal, Université Saint-Joseph – AUPELF-UREF, coll. Universités francophones, pp. 320–338.

Bourdieu, P., 1997, *Méditations pascaliennes*, Paris, Seuil, coll. Liber.

Bourdieu, P., 1992, *Les règles de l'art: Genèse et structure du champ littéraire*, Paris, Seuil.

Bourdieu, P., 1984, *Questions de sociologie*, Paris, Minuit.

Boutin, A. B. & Kouadio, J. N., 2015, 'Le nouchi c'est notre créole en quelque sorte, qui est parlé par presque toute la Côte d'Ivoire', *Dynamique des français africains: entre le culturel et le linguistique*, Peter Blumenthal (Ed.), Berne, Éditions Peter Lang, 2015, pp. 251–271.

Briard, F., 2008, *Tiken Jah Fakoly: l'Afrique ne pleure plus, elle parle*, Paris, Éditions Arènes.

Brou, K. D. (Ed.), 2018a, *Tiken Jah Fakoly: Quand le reggae s'arrime à la pensée. Tome 1. La pensée universitaire*, Paris, L'Harmattan.

Brou, K. D. (Ed.), 2018b, *Tiken Jah Fakoly: Quand le reggae s'arrime à la pensée. Tome 2. Penser et panser l'Afrique*, Paris, L'Harmattan.

Caillé, A., 2007, *Anthropologie du don: Le tiers paradigme*, Paris, La Découverte.

Camara, S, 1992, *Gens de la parole: Essai sur la condition du griot dans la société malinké*, Paris, Karthala.

Castoriadis, C., 1975, *L'institution imaginaire de la société*, Paris, Seuil, coll. Points.

Cauquelin, A., 1999, *Les théories de l'art*, Paris, PUF.

Caune, J., 1995, *Culture et communication: Convergences théoriques et lieux de médiation*, Grenoble, Presses universitaires de Grenoble.

Cissé, Y. T. & Kamissoko, W., 1988, *La grande geste du Mali: Des origines à la fondation de l'empire*, Paris, Association ARSAN.

Collins, J., 1992, *West African Pop Roots*, Philadelphia, Temple University Press.

Coman, M., 2003, *Pour une anthropologie des médias*, Grenoble, Presses universitaires de Grenoble.

Contreras, A., 2016, *Musiques du monde sur Jacques Bizollon*, Radio France internationale https://musique.rfi.fr/emission/info/musiques-monde/20160203-2-jacques-bizollon.

Copans, J., 1993, 'Intellectuels visibles, intellectuels invisibles', *Politique Africaine*, No. 51, pp. 7–25.

Dagri, P., 2019a, 'La fanfare des peuples de la côtière de Côte d'Ivoire: d'hier à aujourd'hui', www.universitepopulairemeroeafrica.org.

Dagri, P., 2019b, 'The sound phenomenon in Africa – music: A semiological approach', www.universitepopulairemeroeafrica.org.

Dédy, S., 1986, 'Vers une définition de l'Art chez les Bété: le mythe de Srèlè', in *La musique populaire en Côte d'Ivoire: Essai sur l'art de Srolou Gabriel*, Christophe Wondji (Ed.), Paris, Présence Africaine, pp. 27–41.

Dédy, S., 1984, 'Musique traditionnelle et développement national en Côte d'Ivoire', *Tiers-Monde*, Vol. 25, No. 97, pp. 109–124; DOI: https://doi.org/10.3406/tiers.1984.3361. www.persee.fr/doc/tiers_0040-7356_1984_num_25_97_3361.

Derrida, J., 1966, *Nature, culture, écriture: La violence de la lettre de Lévi-Strauss à Rousseau*, Paris, ENS, typewritten document. Available at http://cahiers.kingston.ac.uk/vol04/cpa4.1.derrida.html.

Diawarra, M., 2015, 'Breaking the contract? Handling intangible cultural goods among different generations in Mali', in *Copyright Africa: How Intellectual Property, Media and Markets Transform Immaterial Cultural Goods*, Ute Röschenthaler & Mamadou Diawarra (Eds.), Canon Pyon, Sean Kingston Publishing, pp. 242–265.

Djédjé, A.-P., 2020, *L'épopée de la pop music ivoirienne*, Abidjan, Edilis.

Djédjé, N. D., 2005, 'Le développement et la question de l'expression "on est en Afrique". Essai de réflexion psychosociologique sur un facteur idéologique du sous-développement en Afrique', *Kasa Bya Kasa: Revue ivoirienne d'anthrolopologie et de sociologie*, No. 7, pp. 73–86.

Dollfus, O., 2007, *La mondialisation*, Paris, Presses de la fondation nationale des Sciences Politiques.

Doua, E., 2020, 'Reggae, ideologies et luttes émancipatrices en Afrique, *Hermès*, No. 86, pp. 158–163.

Doua, E., 2009, *Les médias dans les politiques culturelles africaines: Le cas du MASA en Côte d'Ivoire*, Doctoral thesis, Bordeaux, Université Michel de Montaigne Bordeaux 3.

Doumergue, D., 1981, 'Essai sur l'alcoolisme en Côte d'Ivoire, 1900–1958', *Annales de l'Université d'Abidjan, Série I (Histoire), Tome IX, pp. 99–120.*

Durkheim, E., 1912[2007], *Les formes élémentaires de la vie religieuse: Le système totémique en Australie*, Paris, CNRS Éditions.

Duvignaud, J., 1991, *Fêtes et civilisations, followed by La fête aujourd'hui*, Paris, Actes Sud.

Eboussi Boulaga, F., 1977, *La crise du muntu: Authenticité africaine et philosophie*, Paris, Présence africaine.

Eza Boto, 1954[1971], *Ville cruelle*, Paris, Présence africaine.

Fanon, F., 1961[2002], *Les damnés de la terre*, Paris, La Découverte.

Farred, G., 2003, *What's My Name? Black Vernacular Intellectuals*, Minneapolis, University of Minnesota Press.

Fié Doh, L., 2012, *Musiques populaires urbaines et stratégies du refus en Côte d'Ivoire*, Paris, Edilivre.

Flichy, P., 2010, *Le sacre de l'amateur: Sociologie des passions ordinaires à l'ère du numérique*, Paris, Seuil.

Flichy, P., 1991, *Les industries de l'imaginaire*, Grenoble, Presses universitaires de Grenoble.

Feld, S., 1988, 'Note on world beat', *Public Culture*, Vol. 1, No. 1, pp. 31–37.

Forest, P.-O., 2013, *Poïétique de la création sonore au cinéma: La figure de l'artiste-poïéticien*, Master's thesis, Université de Montréal.

Fougeyrollas, P., 1987, *Les métamorphoses de la crise: Racismes et révolutions au XXe siècle*, Paris, Hachette.

Gadou, D., 2011, *La sorcellerie: Une réalité vivante en Afrique*, Abidjan, Les éditions du CERAP.

Gibert, G. & Leguern, Ph., 2008, 'Faire l'histoire des musiques amplifiées en France', *Stéréo: Sociologie comparée des musiques populaires, France – Grande-Bretagne*, Guichen, Éditions Mélanie Seteun, Irma, Musique et société/9, DOI: https://doi.org/10.4000/books.ms.405, Publication on OpenEdition Books: 12 September 2019.

Gilroy, P., 2010, *The Black Atlantic: Modernité et double conscience*, Paris, Ed. Amsterdam.

Giddens, A., 1994, *Les conséquences de la modernité*, Paris, L'Harmattan.

Godelier, M., 2015, *L'imaginé, l'imaginaire & le symbolique*, Paris, Cnrs Éditions.

Goerg, O., 1999, 'Introduction', in *Fêtes urbaines en Afrique: Espaces, identités et pouvoirs*, Odile Goerg (Ed.), Paris, Karthala, pp. 5–13.

Goffman, E., 1991, *Les cadres de l'expérience*, Paris, Minuit.

Gondola, Ch. D., 2003, 'Ô, Kisasa makambo! Métamorphoses et représentations de Kinshasa à travers le discours musical des années 1950–1960', *Le Mouvement social* Vol. 3, No. 204, pp. 109–129.

Gondola, Ch. D., 1997, 'Oh rio-Ma! Musique et guerre des sexes à Kinshasa: 1930–1990', *Revue Française d'Histoire d'Outre-Mer*, Vol. 4, No. 314, 1er trim., pp. 51–81.

Goran, K. M. A., 2011, *Musicologie et développement dans la société ivoirienne*, Saarbrücken, Éditions Universitaires Européennes.

Gramsci, A., 1983, *Textes*, Paris, Éditions Sociales.

Grignon, C., 2000, 'L'enquête sociologique, la critique sociale et l'expertise politique', *Revue Européenne des Sciences Sociales*, *XXXVIII-118*, pp. 101–113.

Guébo, J. (Ed.), 2022, *Arafat DJ: Histoire et légende d'une comète*, Paris, L'Harmattan.

Hall, S., 2007, *Identités et cultures: Politique des cultural studies*, edited by Maxime Cervulle, Paris, Éditions Amsterdam.

Hampâté Bâ, A., 1992, *Amkoulel, l'enfant peul*, Paris, Babel.

Hegel, G. W. F., éd.1964, *Introduction à l'esthétique*, Paris, Aubier-Montaigne.

Hennion, A., 1981, *Les professionnels du disque: Une sociologie des variétés*, Paris, Métailié.

Hennion, A. & Latour, A., 1996, L'art, l'aura et la technique selon Benjamin ou comment devenir célèbre en faisant tant d'erreurs à la fois … , *Cahiers de médiologie*, No. 1, pp. 235–241.

Herndon, M., 1992, 'Song', *Folklore, Cultural Performances, and Popular Entertainments: A Communications-Centered Handbook*, Richard Bauman (Ed.), Oxford, Oxford University Press, pp. 159–166.

Hobsbawm, E., 2006[2012], 'Introduction: Inventing Traditions', *The Invention of Tradition*, new expanded edition, Éric Hobsbawm & Terence Ranger (eds.), Paris, Éditions Amsterdam, pp. 27–41.

Kadi, G.-A., 2021, *La révolte du zouglou en Côte d'Ivoire: 30 ans de revendications (1991–2021)*, Paris, L'Harmattan.

Kanga, K. & Goran K. M. A., 2017, *Didactics of music education: De la théorie à la pratique. Tome 1*, Paris, L'Harmattan.

Kebede, A., 1982, *Roots of Black Music: The Vocal, Instrumental and Dance Heritage of Africa and Black America*, Englewood Cliffs, NJ, Prentice Hall.

Kipré, P., 1986, *Villes de Côte d'Ivoire (1893–1940). Tome 2, Économie et société urbaine*, Abidjan, NEA.

Kipré, P., 1985, *Villes de Côte d'Ivoire (1893–1940). Tome 1, La fondation des villes*, Abidjan, NEA.

Kipré, P., 1975, 'La place des centres urbains dans l'économie de la Côte d'Ivoire de 1920 à 1930', *Annales de l'Université d'Abidjan, Série I (Histoire), Tome 3*, pp. 93–120.

Koffi, T., Kipré, A. & N'Ko, L., 2022, *Le grand livre de la musique ivoirienne, tome 1: Alpha Blondy et la galaxie reggae*, Abidjan, Éditions Éburnie.

Kolé, M., 2023, *Ne cherchez pas à comprendre. Dansez seulement! Le Coupé-Décalé et les jeunes en Côte d'Ivoire*, Bamenda, Langaa.

Konaté, Y., 2002, 'Génération zouglou', *Cahiers d'études africaines*, Vol. 168, No. XLII-4, Paris, EHESS, pp. 777–796.

Konaté, Y., 1987, *Alpha Blondy: Reggae et société en Afrique noire*, Paris, Karthala.

Koné, B., 2020, 'La cantatrice Zélé de Papara, une voix au service de la justice et de l'égalité en pays sénoufo', *Droits de l'homme en arts, littératures et sciences humaines en Afrique*, André Banhouman Kamaté (Ed.), Paris, Edilivre, pp. 45–69.

Koné, H., 1989, *La dynamique des médias dans les sociétés en mutations: Le cas de la Côte d'Ivoire*, Thèse de Doctorat d'État, 2t, Strasbourg, Université de Strasbourg.

Kossonou, H., 2020, *La conservation et la transcription des œuvres musicales du service des archives de la documentation générale du BURIDA: Enjeux et perspectives*, doctoral thesis in Art and Culture, Abidjan, INSAAC-IRES-RDEC.

Kouvouama, A., 2013, *Anthropologie de la chanson congolaise de variétés: Imaginaire, production du sens*, Brazzaville – Paris, PAARI.

Kua-Nzambi Toko, A. 2018, 'Musique africaine et répertoire choral', musicologie.org, www.musicologie.org/publirem/musique_africaine_et_repertoire_choral.html.

Laffanour, A., éd., 2003, *Territoires de musiques et cultures urbaines: Rock, rap, techno… l'émergence de la création musicale à l'heure de la mondialisation*, Paris, L'Harmattan.

Lamizet, B., 2002, *Le sens de la ville*, Paris, L'Harmattan.

Latour, B., 2007, *Changer la société, refaire de la sociologie*, Paris, La Découverte/Poche.

Land, Mitchell F., 1995, 'Reggae, resistance and the State: Television and popular music in Côte d'Ivoire', *Critical Studies in Mass Communication*, Vol. 12, No. 4, pp. 438–454 [online 18 May 2009]. https://doi.org/10.1080/15295039509366950.

Land, Mitchell, 1992, 'Ivoirian television, willing vector of cultural imperialism', *Howard Journal of Communications*, Vol. 4, Nos. 1–2, pp. 10–27 [online 27 February 2009]. DOI: https://doi.org/10.1080/10646179209359762.

Laye, C., 1978, *Le maître de la parole: Kouma lafôlô kouma*, Paris, Plon.

Le Pape, M., 1997, *L'énergie sociale à Abidjan: Économie politique de la ville en Afrique noire, 1930–1995*, Paris, Karthala.

Leimdorfer, F., 2006, '"Tu sais, on est en Afrique": Essai d'analyse de séquences discursives orales', *Semen 21* [online 28 April 2007], accessed 9 January 2021. http://journals.openedition.org/semen/1948; DOI: https://doi.org/10.4000/semen.1948.

Lévi-Strauss, C., 1962, *Anthropologie structurale 2*, Paris, Plon.

Lévi-Strauss, C., 1958[1974] , *Anthropologie structurale*, Paris, Plon.

Lyotard, J.-F., 1979, *La condition postmoderne*, Paris, Minuit.

Macamo, E., 2005, 'Introduction. Negotiating modernity: From colonialism to globalization', in *Negotiating Modernity: Africa's Ambivalent Experience*, Elisio Salvado Macamo (Ed.), Dakar-London, Codesria-Z Books, pp. 1–16.

Maffesoli, M., 1988, *Le temps des tribus: Le déclin de l'individualisme dans les sociétés de masse*, Paris, Le Livre de Poche.

Martin, D.-C., 2012, 'The Musical Heritage of Slavery: From Creolization to "World Music"', *Music and Globalization: Critical Encounters*, Bob W. White (Ed.), Bloomington, Indiana University Press, pp. 17–39, accessed 29 October 2020, www.jstor.org/stable/j.ctt16gzm34.5.

Masselis, J., 2016, 'Platon, ou la musique au cœur d'un projet politique', [online] www.francemusique.fr/actualite-musicale/platon-ou-la-musique-au-coeur-d-un-projet-politique-277, accessed 28 February 2020.

Massoumou, O. & Queffélec, A. J.-M., 2007, *Le français en république démocratique du Congo: Sous l'ère multipartiste (1991–2006)*, Paris, Éditions des archives contemporaines.

Mauss, M., 1925[2012], *Essai sur le don: Form and Reason of Exchange in Archaic Societies*, Paris, PUF, Quadrige.

Mazzoleni, F., 2010, 'Les musiques des indépendances africaines', *Africultures* [Online], http://africultures.com/les-musiques-des-independances-africaines-9859/09.08.2018.

Mbembe, J. A., 1985, *Les jeunes et l'ordre politique en Afrique noire*, Paris, L'Harmattan.

Memel-Fotê, H., 1991, 'Des ancêtre fondateurs aux Pères de la nation: Introduction à une anthropologie de la démocratie', XIIIe conférence March Bloch, Paris, Ecole des Hautes Etudes en Sciences Sociales, 18 June 1991; www.ehess.fr/sites/default/files/pagedebase/fichiers/harris_memel-fote.pdf.

Meyer, M., 1997, *Qu'est-ce que la philosophie*, Paris, Livre de poche.

Meyran, R., 2014, 'Les musiques urbaines, ou la subversion des codes esthétiques occidentaux', www.espacestemps.net/articles/les-musiques-urbaines-ou-la-subversion-des-codes-esthetiques-occidentaux/, accessed 9 March 2019.

Mignon, J. M., 1984, *Afrique: Jeunesses uniques, jeunesse encadrée*, Paris, L'Harmattan.

Mkandawire, T., 2005, 'Introduction', *African Intellectuals: Rethinking Politics, Language, Gender and Development*. Thandika Mkandawire (Ed.), pp. 1–9 Dakar: CODESRIA/Zed Books.

Moessinger, P., 2000, *Le jeu de l'identité*, Paris, Presses universitaires de France.

Molino, J., 2009. *Le Singe Musicien: Sémiologie et anthropologie de la musique*, Paris, Actes Sud/INA.

Moreau de Bellaing, L., 1990, *Sociologie de l'autorité*, Paris, L'Harmattan.

Mouchtouris, A., 2007, *Sociologie de la culture populaire*, Paris, L'Harmattan.

Murray Schafer, R., 1979[2010], *The soundscape: Le monde comme musique*, Paris, Wildproject.

Nattiez, J.-J., 2009, 'Introduction à l'œuvre musicologique de Jean Molino', in *Le Singe Musicien: Sémiologie et anthropologie de la musique*, Paris, Actes Sud/INA, pp. 13–70.

N'Da, P., 1999, *Le drame démocratique africain sur scène en Côte d'Ivoire*, Paris, L'Harmattan.

Nganguè, E., 2009, *La musique dans le débat politique et identitaire en Côte d'Ivoire: Le cas du zouglou*, PhD thesis, Paris, École des Hautes Études en Sciences Sociales.

Ngoran, E. Y., 2013, *La rumba congolaise: Sa splendeur, ses effluves, ses profondeurs*, Abidjan, l'Encre Bleue.

Niane, D. T., 1960, *Soundjata ou l'épopée mandingue*, Paris, Présence africaine.

Nyamnjoh, F. B., 2020, 'Manu Dibango: Afropolitan musical genius with a giant heart', https://theconversation.com/manu-dibango-afropolitan-musical-genius-with-a-giant-heart-134679.

Nyamnjoh, F. B., 2019, 'ICTs as Juju: African inspiration for understanding the compositeness of being human through digital technologies', *Journal of African Media Studies*, Vol. 11, No. 3, pp. 279–291.

Nyamnjoh, F. B., 2018, ''Introduction: Cannibalism as food for thought', in *Eating and Being Eaten: Cannibalism as Food for Thought*, Francis B. Nyamnjoh (Ed.), Bamenda, Langaa, pp. 1–98.

Nyamnjoh, F. B., 2017, 'Incompleteness: Frontier Africa and the currency of conviviality', *Journal of Asian and African Studies*, Vol. 52, No. 3, pp. 253–270.

Nyamnjoh, F. B., 2012, '"Potted plants in greenhouses': A critical reflection on the resilience of the colonial education in Africa", *Journal of Asian and African Studies*, Vol. 47, No. 2, pp. 129–154.

Nyamnjoh, F. B. & Fokwang, J., 2005, 'Entertaining repression: Music and politics in postcolonial Cameroon"', *African Affairs*, Vol. 104, No. 415, pp. 251–274.

Olaniyan, T., 2004, *Arrest the Music! Fela and His Rebel Art and Politics*, Bloomington, Indiana University Press.

Olivier, E., 2020, 'Ce que la téléphonie mobile fait à la musique ouest-africaine. Le projet ZikMali: un nouveau modèle de distribution musicale?', *Réseaux*, Vol. 1, No. 219, pp. 71–104, www.cairn.info/revue-reseaux-2020-1-page-71.htm.

Ouattara, I., 2018, 'Le griot dans la société traditionnelle africaine: Patrimoine et survivance d'une conscience d'être et de culture', *International Journal of Latest Research in Humanities and Social Sciences (IJLRHSS)*, Vol. 01, No. 12), pp. 43–52.

Ouattara, A., 1985, 'L'influence des Américains noirs sur les Ivoiriens dans la région d'Abidjan (à travers les mass-médias)', *Kasa Bya Kasa Revue ivoirienne d'anthropologie et de sociologie* No. 7, July/August/September, pp. 70–97.

Ouattara, O. J. & Lasme M. F., 2016, 'La musique islamique en Côte d'Ivoire: Difficultés et conditions d'émergence', *Communication en question*, No. 6, June/July, pp. 22–39.

Paillé, L., 2004, *Livre: La démarche de création*, Trois-Rivières, ed. Le Sabord.

Pajon, L., 2021, 'Il faut rendre à Manu . . .', *Jeune Afrique*, No. 3096, January, pp. 54–55.

Passeron, R., 1999, 'Esthétique et poïétique', *Filozofski vestnik, XX (2/1999 – XIVICA)*, pp. 265–276.

Paturet, J.-B., 2007, 'Qu'est-ce qu'un héritage? Un enjeu pour le travail social de demain', *Empan*, Vol. 4, No. 68, pp. 22–27.

Picton, J., 1992, 'A Tribute to William Fagg, April 28, 1914–July 10, 1992', *African Arts*, Vol. 27, No. 3, Memorial to William Fagg (Jul., 1994), pp. 26–29, www.jstor.org/stable/3337198; accessed 30 August 2019.

Piermay, J.-L., 2003, 'L'apprentissage de la ville en Afrique sud-saharienne', *Le mouvement social*, Vol. 3, No. 204, pp. 35–46, www.cairn.info/revue-le-mouvement-social-2003-3-page-35.htm.

Pierrat, E., 2005, 'How is copyright protected in Africa? An answer from Emmanuel Pierrat, lawyer at the Paris Bar and writer, specialising in intellectual property law', interviewed by Ibrahima Dia, *Jeune Afrique*, 18 July, www.jeuneafrique.com/94652/archives-thematique/comment-est-prot-g-le-droit-d-auteur-en-afrique/.

Plato, 1966, *The Republic*, translation and notes by R. Baccou, Paris, GF Flammarion.

Popovitch, M., 1992, *Tango ya ba Wendo*, documentaire, couleur, 52 minutes, Bruxelles, Atelier Jeunes Cinéastes Ti Suka.

Martin, D.-C., 2000, 'Cherchez le peuple... Culture, populaire et politique', *Critique internationale*, Vol. 7, pp. 169–183.

Retord, G., 1986, 'Les premières projections cinématographiques en Côte d'Ivoire', *Communication Audiovisuelle*, No. 6, pp. 11–31.

Ricci, D., 2016, *Cinémas des diasporas noires: esthétique de la reconstruction*, Paris, L'Harmattan.

Röschenthaler, U., 2015, '"Be faster than the pirates". Copyright and the revival of "traditional dances" in south-west Cameroon', *Copyright Africa: How Intellectual Property, Media and Markets Transform Immaterial Cultural Goods*, Ute Röschenthaler & Mamadou Diawarra (Eds.), Canon Pyon, Sean Kingston Publishing, pp. 177–213.

Roskem, K. J. P., 2014, *L'émergence d'une scène musicale à N'Djaména. Indentification des acteurs et des territoires*, doctoral thesis in information and communication sciences, Avignon, Université d'Avignon et des pays du Vaucluse.

Rouch, J., 1967, *Jaguar*, Paris, Les films de la Pléiade, 35 mm, colour, 110 min.

Rouch, J., 1961, *La pyramide humaine*, Paris, Les films de la Pléiade, 16 mm, black and white, 90 min.

Rouch, J., 1959, *Moi un noir*, Paris, Les films de la Pléiade, 16 mm, colour, 73 min.

Rouch, J., 1955, *Les maîtres fous*, Paris, Les films de la Pléiade, 16 mm, color, 36 min.

Rouzé, V., 2004, *Les musiques diffusées dans les lieux publics: Analyse et enjeux de pratiques communicationnelles quotidiennes*, Doctoral thesis in Information and Communication Sciences, Saint-Denis, Université Paris VIII.

Rowlands, M., 2008, 'Civilization, violence and heritage healing in Liberia', *Journal of Material Culture*, Vol. 13, No. 2, pp. 135–152, DOI: https://10.1177/1359183508090900.

Rowlands, M., 1993, 'The role of memory in the transmission of culture', *World Archeology*, Vol. 5, No. 2, pp. 141–151.

Sadji, A., 1985, *Ce que dit la musique africaine*, Paris, Présence africaine.

Sartre, J.-P., 1972, *Plaidoyer pour les intellectuels*, Paris, Gallimard.

Schechner, R., 2008, *Performance: Expérimentation et théorie du théâtre aux USA*, Montreuil-sous-Bois, Éditions Théâtrales.

Schechner, R., 1985, *Between Theatre and Anthropology*, Philadelphia, University of Pennsylvania Press.

Schütz, A., 2007, *Écrits sur la musique: 1924–1956*, Paris, Editions MF.

Scott, J. C., 2009, *Domination and the Arts of Resistance: Fragments du discours subalterne*, Paris, Éditions Amsterdam.

Segobye, A. K., 2007, 'The gods are resting there: Challenges to the protection of heritage sites through legislation and local knowledge', in *Indigenous Knowledge Systems and Intellectual Property in the Twenty-First Century: Perspectives from Southern Africa*, Isaac Mazondé and Pradip Thomas (Eds.), Dakar, CODESRIA, pp. 78–94.

Séry, B., 2015, *Le Tohourou: Un chemin vers la sagesse*, Abidjan, NEB.

Tacussel, P. & Renard, J.-B., 1998, 'Imaginaire et sociologie', *Introduction aux méthodologies de l'imaginaire*, Joël Thomas (Ed.), Paris, Ellipses, pp. 273–280.

Tapé, G., 1986, 'L'art et l'artiste selon Srolou', *La musique populaire en Côte d'Ivoire: Essai sur l'art de Srolou Gabriel*, Christophe Wondji (Ed.), Paris, Présence Africaine, pp. 137–157.

Tapé, G., 1986b, 'L'art et l'artiste selon Srolou', *La musique populaire en Côte d'Ivoire: Essai sur l'art de Srolou Gabriel*, Christophe Wondji (Ed.), Paris, Présence africaine, pp. 137–157.

Tesser, P., 2006, *Musique, identité et insertion sociale. Mangue Beat: humus culturel*, Thèse de Doctorat en sociologie, Paris, Université Paris-Descartes.

Thomas, J., 1998, 'Introduction', *Introduction aux méthodologies de l'imaginaire*. Joël Thomas (Ed.), Paris, Ellipses, pp. 15–21.

Thomas, P. & Nyamnjoh, F., 2007, 'Intellectual property challenges in Africa: Indigenous knowledge systems and the fate of connected worlds', in *Indigenous Knowledge Systems and Intellectual Property in the Twenty-First Century: Perspectives from Southern Africa*, Isaac Mazonde & Pradip Thomas (Eds.), Dakar, Codesria, pp. 12–25.

Titon, T. J., 1992, 'Music, folk and traditional', in *Folklore, Cultural Performances, and Popular Entertainments: A Communications-Centered Handbook*, Richard Bauman (Ed.), Oxford, Oxford University Press, pp. 167–171.

Toulabor, C., 1993, 'Masque errant?', *Politique africaine*, No. 51, pp. 3–6.

Touré, A., 1981, *La civilisation quotidienne en Côte d'Ivoire: Procès d'occidentalisation*, Paris, Karthala.

Traoré, R., 1986, 'La distribution cinématographique en Côte d'Ivoire', *Communication Audiovisuelle*, No. 6, pp. 195–225.

Tudesq, A.-J., 2002, *L'Afrique parle, l'Afrique écoute: Les radios en Afrique subsaharienne*, Paris, Karthala.

Tudesq, A.-J., 1999, *Les médias en Afrique*, Paris, Ellipses.

Tudesq, A.-J., 1998, *Journaux et radios d'Afrique aux XIXe et XXe siècles*, Paris, GRET.

Turner, V., 1988, *The Anthropology of Performance*, New York, PAJ Publications.

Turner, V., 1969[1997], *The Ritual Process: Structure and Anti-structure*, New Brunswick-London, Aldine Transaction.

Van Gennep, A., 1909[1981], *Les rites de passage: Étude systématique des rites*, Paris, Picard.

Vian, B., 1958[1997], *En avant la zizique*, Paris, Le livre de poche.

Vidal, C., 2002, 'Abidjan, ville-monde (1957–2000)', *Les temps modernes* 2002/4–5, Nos. 620–621, pp. 463–479.

Vidal, C., 1992, *Sociologie des passions: Rwanda, Côte d'Ivoire*, Paris, Karthala.

Vergès, G., 2018, *Magic System: Le mystère 1er Gaou*, Paris, Les éditions du Panthéon.

Warnier, J.-P., 2007, *La mondialisation de la culture*, Paris, La Découverte, 4th ed.

Warnier, J.-P., 1994, 'Introduction: Six objets en quête d'authenticité', in *Le paradoxe de la marchandise authentique: Imaginaire et consommation de masse*, Jean-Pierre Warnier (Ed.), Paris, L'Harmattan, pp. 11–34.

Waterman, C. A., 1990, '"Our tradition is a very modern tradition": Popular music and the construction of Pan Yoruba identity', *Ethnomusicology*, Vol. 34, No. 3 (autumn), pp. 367–379, www.jstor.org/stable/851623, accessed 26/06/2014 23:42.

Weaver, W., 1949, 'Recent contributions to the mathematical theory of communication', in *The Mathematical Theory of Communication*. Claude Shannon & Warren Weaver (Eds.), pp. 94–117, Urbana, The University of Illinois Press.

Weber, M., 1971[1995], *Economie et société 1: Les catégories de la société*, Paris, Plon-Pocket, coll. Agora.

Winkin, Y., 2001, *Anthropologie de la communication: De la théorie au terrain*, Paris, Seuil, coll. Points Essais.

Wolikow, S., 1998, 'L'histoire du temps présent en question', *Territoires contemporains*, special issue no. 5, pp. 9–24.

Wondji, C., 1986a, 'Chanson et culture populaire en Côte d'Ivoire', in *La musique populaire en Côte d'Ivoire: Essai sur l'art de Srolou Gabriel*, Christophe Wondji (Ed.), Paris, Présence Africaine, pp. 11–24.

Wondji, C., 1986b, 'Le bagnon et l'art', in *La musique populaire en Côte d'Ivoire: Essai sur l'art de Srolou Gabriel*, Christophe Wondji (Ed.), Paris, Présence Africaine, pp. 42–83.

Yapi Diahou, A., 2000, *Baraques et développement dans l'agglomération d'Abidjan*, Paris, L'Harmattan.

Zadi, Z. B., 1990, 'Introduction à la connaissance de la poésie orale de Côte d'Ivoire', *Annales de l'Université d'Abidjan: Traditions orales*, Vol. 5, pp. 5–44.

Zadi, Z. B., 1977, 'Regard sur l'œuvre poétique de Nahounou Digbeu (Amédée Pierre)', *Bissa: Revue Littéraire Orale,* No. 6, Abidjan, GRTO.

Zang Zang, P., 2018, 'Du français en Afrique au(x) français d'Afrique: Quel(s) parcours?', in *Aspects linguistiques et sociolinguistiques des français africains*, Oreste Floquet (Ed.), Roma, Sapientia Università Editrice, pp. 1–20.

Zeleza, P. T., 2005, 'The academic diaspora and knowledge production in and on Africa: What role for CODESRIA?', in *African Intellectuals: Rethinking Politics, Language, Gender and Development*. Thandika Mkandawire (Ed.), pp. 209–234. Dakar, CODESRIA/Zed Books.

Zemp, H., 1971[2012], *Musique Dan: Music in the Thought and Social Life of an African Society*, Berlin, De Gruyter, digital reprint (original: Paris-La Haye, Mouton-EPHE).

Cambridge Elements ≡

Critical Heritage Studies

Kristian Kristiansen
University of Gothenburg

Michael Rowlands
UCL

About the Series

This series focuses on the recently established field of Critical Heritage Studies. Interdisciplinary in character, it brings together contributions from experts working in a range of fields, including cultural management, anthropology, archaeology, politics, and law. The series will include volumes that demonstrate the impact of contemporary theoretical discourses on heritage found throughout the world, raising awareness of the acute relevance of critically analysing and understanding the way heritage is used today to form new futures.

Cambridge Elements ≡

Critical Heritage Studies

www.ingramcontent.com/pod-product-compliance
Lightning Source LLC
LaVergne TN
LVHW010144141224
799073LV00004B/477

* 9 7 8 1 0 0 9 4 6 9 1 6 6 *

Shaftesbury Road, Cambridge CB2 8EA, United Kingdom

One Liberty Plaza, 20th Floor, New York, NY 10006, USA

477 Williamstown Road, Port Melbourne, VIC 3207, Australia

314–321, 3rd Floor, Plot 3, Splendor Forum, Jasola District Centre, New Delhi – 110025, India

103 Penang Road, #05–06/07, Visioncrest Commercial, Singapore 238467

Cambridge University Press is part of Cambridge University Press & Assessment, a department of the University of Cambridge.

We share the University's mission to contribute to society through the pursuit of education, learning and research at the highest international levels of excellence.

www.cambridge.org
Information on this title: www.cambridge.org/9781009469180

DOI: 10.1017/9781009469159

© Aghi Bahi 2024

When citing this work, please include a reference to the DOI 10.1017/9781009469159

First published 2024

A catalogue record for this publication is available from the British Library.

ISBN 978-1-009-46918-0 Hardback
ISBN 978-1-009-46916-6 Paperback
ISSN 2632-7074 (online)
ISSN 2632-7066 (print)